All In

All In

You, Your Business, Your Life

Arlene Dickinson

Collins

This book is dedicated to all entrepreneurs—those who are just starting out, those who are well established, and those who claim to be retired (but are actually busy doing things on the side)— and their families, whose support makes the journey not only possible but worthwhile. May all your dreams come true.

Contents

Introduction

Entrepreneurship isn't a job. It's a demanding, rewarding, scary, thrilling, and ultimately all-encompassing lifestyle. For entrepreneurs, the conventional divisions between work life and home life, family finances and business finances, don't exist. Work, money, and relationships are all connected for us, and at one point or another they've all been on the line. We cash in our savings, we talk business at the dinner table, we check our smartphones at the beach, we put our houses up as collateral. Again, and again, and again. To be an entrepreneur is to pursue a dream with everything you have and all that you are. There are no half-measures. You have to be all in. And that level of commitment will test your inner strength more than you ever imagined, and more than you sometimes think you can bear.

Years ago a client invited me to a dinner party at his sprawling Calgary home. There were 12 of us at the table that night, but I was the only entrepreneur. The rest of the guests were executives running large corporations worth hundreds of millions of dollars.

Venture Communications, the marketing company I founded with partners about a decade earlier, was on the rise. But in the world of these high-powered CEOs, my company was a small fish.

When the conversation turned to business, I stiffened up. As others discussed the sorts of challenges that billion-dollar corporations face, I badly wanted to contribute. After all—I was in business, too. But their problems—unfavourable exchange rates, fluctuating commodity prices, HR systems for 10,000-plus employees—simply didn't apply to an independent marketing company like mine. I was still embroiled in the day-to-day challenges of the entrepreneur: pounding the pavement for new clients, wooing banks for expansion loans, and hiring the very best people I could without blowing my HR budget. I was incredibly proud of myself and of my company. But as I sat there, surrounded by wood-panelled walls, fine crystal, and business talk that sailed right over my head, I experienced a crippling case of mini-me syndrome. I was a kid at the grown-ups' table: out of my league and dumbstruck. I sipped my wine, zipped my lips, and prayed I could get through the entire meal without sounding too naive.

I'll never forget the moment when one of the CEOs eventually turned to me and said, "So, Arlene, what do *you* do?" Eleven pairs of eyes watched me. I tried to keep my voice steady and speak loud enough so they could actually hear me. "I'm an entrepreneur," I said. But it didn't sound like a bold, brave statement. It sounded more like an apology.

My inability to confidently and proudly declare who I was and what I did bothered me deeply. My fellow guests had the systems, processes, and resources of huge corporations backing them up. And while I had a great team and some solid revenue to my credit, I knew that, when push came to shove, the only person I had backing me up was me. And in that moment, that knowledge made me feel as small, weak, and insecure as I'd ever felt in my life. I didn't realize back then that I wasn't alone and that most entrepreneurs must at one point or another contend with the same bouts of vicious self-doubt I felt that night. I also didn't realize how destructive this inner conflict can be, not only to entrepreneurs themselves, but also to their families and their businesses.

Inside the heart of every entrepreneur is a tug-of-war between surging confidence and bouts of self-doubt. Entrepreneurs live in the realm of what *might* be possible. We crave opportunity, flexibility, and the ability to build. Which means that whether you're just starting out in business or launching your fifth company, fear and self-doubt are ever-present. Facing this uncertainty day after day takes tremendous emotional resilience. If you aren't mentally prepared to face the challenges that go hand in hand with entrepreneurship, you may, like me at that Calgary dinner party, begin to doubt yourself and the unique skill set you offer the world. That's a huge problem, because when you're an entrepreneur the cornerstone of the business is *you*. And sadly, you're usually the most neglected resource in your business. By a long shot.

That's why I wrote this book. There are plenty of great books out there about how to run a company, but there isn't as much information on how to build the inner strength you need to succeed as an entrepreneur. These inner obstacles are every bit as important to entrepreneurial success as financing, marketing, or operations. The importance of building your inner entrepreneurial skills can't be overstated. The more you grow, the more you need these skills. They are aspects of your business you'll never be able to outsource no matter how successful you are.

All In is about the inner and personal fundamentals you need to cultivate in order to succeed as an entrepreneur. These fundamentals apply whether you're just starting out in business or you're a serial entrepreneur, preparing to throw down the gauntlet yet again. The principles never get old. And for better or worse, you never stop needing them.

During my first few years in business, I was often afraid that we wouldn't be able to make payroll. I'd think about what would happen to me if the business failed: personal humiliation and financial ruin. Back then, I assumed my fears would disappear as I became more successful. They didn't. While I no longer worry about making payroll or losing my house, I have an entirely new set of worries that are every bit as scary: Will YouInc, an online platform company I've recently launched, hit its financial targets? Will the companies I'm involved in continue to grow? How can I ensure Venture Communications maintains its growth trajectory? Have I thought through the details of a new deal carefully enough? Should I invest in a potentially lucrative new venture, even though it's in an industry I know little about?

I understand that all entrepreneurs face fear, uncertainty, and self-doubt. But I've developed the mental muscles I need to protect myself against those feelings. This isn't the case for everyone. I have witnessed first-hand the hazards of trying to embrace the entrepreneurial lifestyle without the inner strength to underwrite it. From addiction and broken relationships to failed businesses and bankruptcy, the personal toll of the entrepreneurial life can be devastating when you're not emotionally prepared to withstand the challenges. That's the bad news. The good news, however, is that the emotional fundamentals you need to succeed as an entrepreneur can all be developed. I learned these skills the old-fashioned way—by making mistakes. By sharing these lessons with you, I hope to help you hone your emotional reserves and save you from making quite as many missteps as I did.

Can You Learn to Be an Entrepreneur?

I didn't get involved in my first business until I was 31, an age when many people are already well established in their careers. Up to that point, I'd been at home raising my kids and working in a series of dead-end jobs. But the moment I started building Venture Communications with my then partners, I knew I'd discovered my true calling. Something that had been inside me for as long as I could remember—a driven, creative, productive instinct—roared to life. And it's been burning in my gut ever since.

Looking back on my early adulthood I see that, while I didn't own a business, I had always lived in an entrepreneurial way. The energy that helped me build Venture into one of Canada's largest independent marketing companies was the same energy I'd needed as a stay-at-home mother cooking soups, baking pies, and canning vegetables from my garden. It's not that I loved doing these things (though the smell of a fresh-baked apple pie is its own kind of heaven). I gardened, baked, and canned because we were broke and I saw an opportunity to save money and eat healthy. It was an entrepreneurial decision.

Later, when I applied that same drive in the workforce while supporting my then husband to go to school, I was less successful. I worked hard, but my desire to find new and better ways of doing things was mistaken for insubordination. My drive to succeed was viewed as threatening and uppity. Today, I see in my younger self the classic struggle of the entrepreneur trying to make it in a corporate system that constricts our need for independence and room to manoeuvre. But back then, I felt frustrated, hemmed in, and underappreciated. Sometimes I even felt ashamed about my inability to play a game I didn't understand. I thought something was wrong with me.

Get Used to Being Misunderstood

The feeling of "wrongness" I describe above is something many entrepreneurs can relate to. Lots of us have experienced the sting of getting fired from a job for being hard to manage, or being told by people we love and respect that our dreams are impractical and irresponsible. It doesn't help that the world is chock full of stereotypes about entrepreneurs: we're always looking to make a buck, we couldn't hack it in the corporate world, we lavish more attention on our businesses than our relationships, we're so blinded by our dreams that we'll sacrifice anything—including our family's financial future—to make them happen.

Are we guilty of these so-called sins? Absolutely. Ask anyone close to an entrepreneur and they'll tell you we do all these things again and again. But the problem with stereotypes isn't that they're untrue. It's that they're half-true. Entrepreneurs are not reckless risk-takers. In fact, this stereotype of the addicted-to-risk entrepreneur is probably the most damaging of all. What better way to snuff out the entrepreneurial spark than to suggest you can't be an entrepreneur *and* a caring, responsible person? And what better way to erode the inner resources entrepreneurs need in order to succeed? Entrepreneurs care deeply—so deeply that we're willing to take risks others wouldn't take in order to build a better future for our families and the people who work for us.

Our inherent understanding of the connection between risk and reward—and our unique ability to comprehend and mitigate that risk—makes us entrepreneurs. And when our calculated risks pay off, the rewards extend far beyond simply making us richer. We create jobs, support families, contribute to social systems through taxes, and create a culture of creativity and innovation. Building all that from scratch takes everything you've got and then some. Many people don't understand this commitment and, as entrepreneurs, we're often judged harshly by ourselves and others for making the sacrifices our path requires of us. That, too, is something that both established and budding entrepreneurs need to anticipate and prepare for. Because when you erode the cornerstone of your business—*you*—you may wake up one day to find there is little left.

A few years ago, a group of girlfriends and I planned a cooking holiday in Italy. It was my dream trip and I thought I'd accounted for every detail. The preparations had been under way for months. Our flights and hotel reservations were booked, and we'd paid the enrolment fees for the cooking school. An acquisition deal I'd been working on for half a year was wrapping up on schedule. Everything was working out according to plan. When I went to sleep, I found myself dreaming of fresh pasta and good red wine.

But a week before we were scheduled to leave for Rome, I hit a roadblock in my negotiations with the company I was acquiring. The deal had to be restructured, and quickly. I worked around the clock with my team to hammer out a new agreement. We were making good progress, so I didn't say anything to my girlfriends. I'd had to cancel so many coffee dates, dinner parties, and holidays with them in the past that I was determined to see this trip through. But coming to a new agreement took longer than expected. Two days before we were supposed to leave, I called my friends and told them I couldn't go to Italy. I gave the trip to the sister of one of the friends who was going and stayed home to finish the deal.

If this had happened 20 years earlier, when I was just beginning to understand what it means to be an entrepreneur, I'd have been wracked by guilt. But as terrible as it sounds, I've learned that blowing off dates with friends on account of last-minute business brush fires comes with the territory for entrepreneurs. We accept this whole-hog attitude from people in other professions. No one questions an emergency room doctor who works past the end of his shift to help a patient. We don't question the farmer who misses her son's basketball game because it's milking time. But entrepreneurs often face criticism for doing what we need to do to build our businesses. And for me, in this instance the thing I had to do was cancel a much-anticipated holiday with my friends. They were bitterly disappointed and I felt like an awful friend for letting them down. But I was also thrilled to have closed the deal. And a week later, when I celebrated the acquisition with my team at Venture, the culinary trip to Italy was the furthest thing from my mind—although I did find time later to ensure our friendship stayed strong.

Light the Fire

I don't know of any entrepreneurs who haven't experienced the guilt and inner conflict I felt in the moments before I called my friends to cancel the trip. Those temporary stabs of regret and uncertainty don't go away, no matter how successful you become or how many businesses you've successfully launched. As an entrepreneur, you're often torn between your passion for what you do, your responsibilities to the people you love, and the risks you have to take to achieve your dreams. It's not an easy path, and you'll have to walk most of it alone. Very often, the only thing to nourish you and light your way will be the fire in your belly.

I can't create that fire for you. What I *can* help with is outlining what to expect from the entrepreneurial lifestyle: the bumps in the road that might trip you up and the obstacles to avoid—all the "personal" stuff no one talks about in most business books. In my opinion, these things are even more crucial than being able to write a business plan or read a balance sheet. The miscalculations many entrepreneurs make, the ones that derail their companies, are not financial. They're emotional. These entrepreneurs find out the hard way that they weren't, in fact, ready to go all in—they had no realistic idea of what independence feels like or what it costs.

For entrepreneurs, the personal *is* professional. The defining feature of the lifestyle is that there is no dividing line, no real boundary, between the two spheres. Work is life. Life is work. That can be wonderful and energizing and make you both happy and successful. Or it can ruin you, if you're unable to adapt to what is essentially a radically different way of life. The key is expecting those differences and preparing for them.

I've come a long way emotionally from that Calgary dinner party. By understanding and applying the inner fundamentals I lay out in this book, I've been able to embrace the challenges inherent in the lifestyle. Thanks to my work on *Dragons' Den*, it's rare that people ask me what I do for a living anymore. But if someone were to ask, I'd tell them with pride, humility, and deep passion that I'm an entrepreneur.

I want you to harness that same power, conviction, and confidence—without all the missteps I made along the way. Let's get started.

Chapter 1

Born This Way

Are you born an entrepreneur? Or is entrepreneurship a set of skills you develop over time? For success in business, the answer is both. If you don't have an innate talent for entrepreneurship, all the hard work in the world won't bring you the success you dream about. I often meet people who either have a great business idea or are in love with the idea of entrepreneurship, but lack the personal characteristics they need for the lifestyle: an appetite for independence in every facet of their lives and the emotional aptitude to deal with the consequences, professionally and personally. Figuring out if you have what it takes is an important first step for budding entrepreneurs. And for a seasoned entrepreneur, it never hurts to check in to make sure the characteristics that first drove you to this lifestyle are still alive and kicking.

It took me a long time to hit my entrepreneurial stride. If you were to look at my life 25 years ago, you wouldn't think I was a born entrepreneur. Back then I was a timid young woman, unsure of myself in many ways, and no one would have confused me with a business dynamo or budding venture capitalist.

Compare that to Vancouver entrepreneur Charles Chang, who at age seven made up stickers proclaiming, "Charles Chang, CEO." (They're still stuck on the walls of his childhood bedroom.) Talk about predicting the future—today, he's the founder and CEO of Vega, a manufacturer of plant-based supplements, which does roughly $72 million in annual sales. Charles started his first "business" before he was even in school, making comic books and selling them to neighbourhood kids for two bucks a pop. By age 10, he had three paper routes. And by the time he was old enough to ride the bus alone, he had parlayed a love of fishing into a thriving cash business. On Saturdays he would take a net and a bucket to the Vancouver coast, where he'd spend the morning catching sunfish. When he had a bucketful, he'd hop back on the bus and stop in at all three of the city's aquariums, where he'd sell the fish for five dollars apiece. "I was the guy who always won the chocolate bar–selling contest at school. I just had this drive inside me—I always looked for ways to make money."

From the outside, Charles's entrepreneurial journey couldn't be further from my own. His money-making instincts kicked in early, while mine took longer to surface. But on the inside? Well, that's a whole different story. One thing we both had from an early age was a fierce desire for independence and a need to strike out on our own. As entrepreneurs, we may not come from the womb knowing how to turn a profit, and we may not all be able to predict at age seven that we're going to be CEO one day. But if there's one thing I've learned in 25 years of being an entrepreneur and working with many others, it's this: we are almost certainly born with a particular kind of spirit.

The "No" Problem

If you're a born entrepreneur, you probably never felt comfortable going with the flow. Even as a child, you were likely trying to control the tide of conformity. Tony Lacavera certainly was. He is one of the most independent-minded people I know. When he started WIND Mobile, Canada's first new national wireless carrier in a decade, he had to contend with loads of opposition from the country's telecommunications giants. After he stepped down in January 2013, he went on to do something that was just as challenging—launch Globalive Capital, a venture fund that invests in domestic technology, media, and telecom companies. In both cases he dealt with plenty of naysayers who told him that his dreams simply weren't possible. But he's used to facing resistance because he has been questioning conventional wisdom and trying to do things his own way his whole life.

At the age of six, he became fixated on the idea of getting past the fence between his backyard and his neighbour's. Walking around would be just too easy—what would be the fun in that? Instead, he jerry-rigged a ladder and climbed over. When his mother discovered what he'd done, she banned further climbing on the quite reasonable grounds that she didn't want him to fall and break his neck. So Tony found a toy shovel and spent the next three weeks digging a trench *underneath* the fence.

As Tony's story suggests, the desire to be an entrepreneur—which is, essentially, the desire to do things your own way paired with the stubborn conviction that you should never stop trying—seems to be innate and often reveals itself pretty early on in life. (Think of Charles Chang's two-dollar comic books.) That's certainly what most of the 200 US entrepreneurs surveyed by Northeastern University's School of Technological

Entrepreneurship told researchers. They conceded that, yes, the practical business skills required to launch a venture can be learned, but about two-thirds of respondents said natural desire— not necessity, not training, not a cratering economy—was what drove them to call on those skills in the first place by starting entrepreneurial ventures. Only one percent said higher education had motivated them at all. In fact, most were aware of their desire long before they got out of high school. Some 42 percent launched their first business ventures in childhood and, significantly, the vast majority of them felt confident they would succeed. In other words, from the time they were kids, they thought, behaved, and *felt* like entrepreneurs.

Those statistics don't mean that if you didn't start a website when you were in kindergarten, you're temperamentally ill-suited to becoming an entrepreneur. Like I said—I didn't start a business when I was a child, either. Instead, I got married— at 19!—and started having babies. But like Tony, I always had a stubborn independent streak, and I was hell-bent on doing things my own way.

One of the first jobs I got after graduating high school was as an administrative assistant at a university. My fellow employees spent their time doing what our boss hired them to do— answer phones, file documents, type up correspondence, and so on. But I thought I would be able to contribute *more* by having in-depth conversations with my co-workers, my boss's colleagues, and pretty much everyone else I worked with in order to develop stronger relationships with the team and get a better understanding of how my work fit into the bigger picture. It's not that I was avoiding my duties; I was simply trying to redefine my job description in a way that allowed me to add as much value as

I could. But my boss—who had hired a secretary because that's precisely what she needed—viewed my tactics as insubordinate and fired me.

I never saw the value of following what I viewed as pointless rules, so I was a terrible employee, forever questioning authority and coming up with my own bright ideas about how to do things better. Looking back, I can see that I had the spirit of an entrepreneur. I just didn't know what to call it back then or what do with it.

Entrepreneurs are not unlike singers, artists, or other creative types in one important respect: we view what we do as a calling. Our work is far more than a job. It's a passion, a way of life that both defines and expresses who we are. It doesn't feel optional, because we can't imagine doing anything else and being happy. A lot of us have tried working for other people. But we're either lousy at it or dissatisfied with it, or both. "It's not a good fit," as I was repeatedly told when I was being fired. Striving for independence, even though it's difficult and involves insecurity and risk, just *feels* better—so much better that it seems like the only choice.

Of course, the price of your fierce independence is that you're often left facing challenges alone, especially early on when you haven't yet built a team to support you. It's not easy, believe me. Having inspirational mentors or supportive friends and family members can be a godsend. But you can survive and thrive without them, so long as you have an entrepreneurial temperament. All of us have something to prove, generally, and "no" isn't just a word we don't like to hear—it's an aphrodisiac that makes us fall even more in love with our own vision and venture.

A Rebel Heart

It helps to be a rebel at heart, one who instinctively questions the status quo. Most successful entrepreneurs are naturally oppositional. We were the kids who drove our parents crazy by always asking, "But why not?" As adults, nothing strengthens our resolve quite like hearing that we have to do something—or *can't* do something. We hate being boxed in.

When I was little, my dad nicknamed me "yeahbut" for reasons that are probably obvious. I always insisted on looking for a way around any parental objection or explanation. I know my dad admired that quality in the abstract—he viewed it as a sign of independent thinking—but day to day, it drove him nuts that I never simply accepted that the answer to a question couldn't be challenged.

That's typical of entrepreneurs, who cheerfully refuse to accept the argument that just because something hasn't been done before, or is difficult, or looks impossible, it's not worth trying.

For the most part, this drive reveals itself early. For instance, when seafood magnate John Risley was 10 years old, the headmaster at his Halifax school asked him what he was going to be when he grew up. "A millionaire," was John's reply. The headmaster laughed off his response and instructed young John to quit dreaming and start focusing on more practical matters—like his schoolwork. "At that point, I had one of two choices," says John, the co-founder of Clearwater Seafoods, whose 2012 net worth was pegged by *Canadian Business* at $910 million. "I could accept that what the headmaster said was the truth and subvert my dreams accordingly. Or I could decide that I wasn't going to let anyone tell me what I could and could not do. I chose the latter."

Rebelling against the advice of authority figures is a recurring theme in many entrepreneurs' backstories. Take Tim Moore, who has built several multi-million-dollar businesses, including AMJ Campbell moving company and Premier Executive Suites, both of which are among the largest businesses in Canada in their categories. Pretty impressive for a kid who was labelled a jock and a ne'er do well in school. After Tim failed three grades, some of his teachers discouraged him from applying to university because he "didn't have the aptitude for academics." But this lack of faith in Tim's intelligence didn't discourage him, it enraged him—then it inspired him to prove them wrong. He successfully applied to university, majored in history, and went on to earn a master's degree—in education. After he graduated, he went on to teach junior high school for several years before quitting to launch his career as an entrepreneur. To this day, Tim still feels the burn of his teachers' slight. "I have never ever liked anyone telling me what I can and cannot do."

Entrepreneurs are always looking for a way around "no, never, forget it, not going to happen." It's not that we're driven to prove others wrong. Oh, okay, sometimes we are—the desire to "show" the skeptics can be highly motivating. Take John Risley's barely contained glee when he tells the headmaster story, as an example. But what drives us is something far more intrinsic. We're motivated by a desire to prove something to ourselves. "It's a disease—this never-ending desire to build something that didn't exist before," says John. Because that drive is internal and comes from somewhere deep inside, it's a bottomless well to draw from. Most entrepreneurs I know don't become *less* entrepreneurial as they age. They become even more so.

A Teflon Will

Something else an entrepreneur is born with: a Teflon will. No matter how much success you achieve, or how many businesses you build and sell, it's not all good all the time—just ask anyone who lives with an entrepreneur, or anyone who's invested in one of our failed ventures. Your Teflon will is what enables you not only to withstand the small-scale rejections and emotional challenges that hit you on a daily basis, but also to stay quick-witted and even-keeled in the midst of them.

This mental toughness gets stronger over time, but it's something most entrepreneurs are born with. In my case, it showed up long before I had a business. I have always been a neat freak and I take great pleasure in good, homemade food. Both require huge amounts of time, energy, and persistence. Even when my four kids were small and I was changing two dozen diapers a day, dealing with toddler meltdowns, and playing blocks, Barbies, and toy soldiers, we always had a clean house and fresh-baked bread. Like most parents, I was exhausted and sleep-deprived when my kids were small. I didn't always *want* to clean and bake, even though both jobs were important to me. But I had a powerful drive and inner strength that gave me the energy to accomplish what I set out to do.

Today, I apply those same mental reserves in my business life. You've probably heard the horror stories about entrepreneurs clawing their way back from near bankruptcy or, through the start-up phase, operating on less sleep than the parents of a colicky newborn. I've been there, and I've got plenty of battle scars to show for it. But for many of us seasoned entrepreneurs, it's not the occasional near catastrophes that take the biggest emotional toll—it's the daily ups and downs that can test our resolve.

I can remember sitting down for a one-on-one meeting in Calgary with the CEO of a multi-billion-dollar energy company. This was about 10 years into my career with Venture; the company was on the rise, and I'd had many such strategy meetings before. But on this particular morning, about halfway through our meeting, the magnitude of what I was doing—advising one of the most powerful people I had ever met on his communications strategy—hit me like a boot to the chest. My brain flooded with self-doubt: *Who do you think you are? Why should he listen to you? What are you even doing here in the first place?* Meanwhile, the nature of our discussion meant that I had to pull on all my inner smarts, experiences, and resources to give him the insight he needed while my interior monologue droned on in the background. This is where my Teflon will kicked in and allowed me to ace the session in spite of the crippling insecurity I was experiencing on the inside. At the end of the meeting, the CEO congratulated me on my work and followed my advice. I walked out of his office elated that I had been able to pull it off without breaking into a sweat—at least not one that he could see.

If any of this—the stubbornness, the fundamental optimism, the resilience, the insistence on self-direction—sounds familiar, you've either already committed to the life of the entrepreneur or you have the temperament of one. Do you have the appetite to become one? That's a risk I hope this book helps you calculate. Maybe you crave independence but just haven't found the idea that ignites your passion. Maybe you're an "intrepreneur"—someone trying to revolutionize a company from within. Or maybe you're just not sure yet how to follow your heart's desire. You can't figure out where the path starts or you think you're too young, or too old, to get started.

Were You Born Here?

It's hard to talk about born entrepreneurs without talking about people who take perhaps the biggest risk of all—leaving the place they grew up in to start a new life somewhere else. I immigrated to Canada from South Africa when I was a child and, in my experience, many of Canada's top entrepreneurs are immigrants. So it didn't surprise me to read in *Maclean's* last year that close to 20 percent of self-employed Canadians were not born in this country. Research suggests that immigrants are more inclined to innovate than the native-born are because they have less to lose and fewer ties to traditional cultural assumptions about how things should be done. And, unfortunately, sometimes the driver is discrimination: if you can't find a decent job because of your accent or your ethnic background, you may be more driven to create your own opportunities. Many immigrants are forced to get creative. Initially, it's a matter of survival.

Media mogul Salah Bachir's father closed down a large contracting company in Lebanon to move his five children to Toronto, where he felt they'd have a better life. Salah's father got a job as a welder, and the children adjusted to a working-class upbringing in their new country. To this day, Salah has vivid memories of his mom and dad attending parent-teacher meetings at schools and doing their best to get their points across in halting English. Seeing the sacrifices his parents made gave Salah a burning desire to make their hardships worth the struggle. After graduating from university, Salah started working in his brother's video rental business, where he launched a monthly newsletter about upcoming home rental releases. The brothers built up the company, and today Salah is president of Cineplex Media, a cinema-marketing company. "I think a lot of immigrant kids want to prove to their parents that they made the right move. So they try harder than anybody else. I've seen that in my own life, and I've seen it with friends as well."

Emotionally, you have to be pretty tough and fearless to be willing to leave everything behind, including your own language, in pursuit of the dream of a better life. You have to be prepared to work hard, make sacrifices, and live by your wits. What's particularly interesting to me is that a lot of first-generation Canadians I meet don't even think of themselves as particularly entrepreneurial. They think of what they're doing as a way of putting food on the table, not as a manifestation of a burning desire for independence. They have adapted so well to self-reliance that it's like oxygen—invisible but necessary, and no big deal.

The "How" of It

The good news is that there's no set path to becoming an entrepreneur. That's part of the beauty of it. Similar themes emerge when entrepreneurs tell you their creation stories, but each story is a little different.

Some people recognize early on that they're simply not made to follow a conventional course, and they never even bother trying. As reported in *Rolling Stone* magazine, Bob Dylan dropped out of his freshman year of college and left Hibbing, Minnesota, at 19 with little more than a few dollars in his pocket, an unflinching belief in his own talent, and a sense that he was destined to follow a particular path. Arriving in New York in a driving blizzard, not knowing a soul, he trekked 40 blocks to Greenwich Village and asked if he could perform at one of the coffeehouses that night. He got the gig, then slept on friends' couches or rode the subway all night until he was discovered.

Bud Kirchner—who, as founder of Kirchner Private Capital Group, has helped hundreds of start-ups get off the ground—likes to say that you know you're an entrepreneur if you actually *made* money in university. Cactus Club Cafe founder Richard Jaffray sure did—before he dropped out of university to pursue his entrepreneurial dreams. He was in his second year of an engineering degree at the University of Calgary when some classmates invited him on an epic month-long surfing trip in Hawaii. Then a penniless student, he and a friend decided to throw a huge party to raise money for the trip. They hired a DJ, rented space, bought a keg, and applied a cover charge. The next morning, after they'd paid their bills, they found they'd cleared $1,800, which in the mid-1980s was more than enough to cover airfare, accommodation, and food. It wasn't Richard's first taste of entrepreneurship; as a kid he'd had several lemonade stands and even started a business buying candies in bulk, packaging them as singles, and selling them on the street for a profit. But his party-for-profit experience in Calgary was a reminder of just how natural it felt to him to create his own opportunities. When he returned from Hawaii, Richard dropped out of university, moved to Vancouver, and lived in his car for a few months while he waited tables and gathered enough money to open his first restaurant. Over the next two decades, he parlayed his first café into a chain of restaurants. Today, there are roughly two dozen Cactus Club Cafe restaurants throughout Alberta, British Columbia, and Ontario.

*   *   *

Not all entrepreneurs find their feet so early in life. They may lack the confidence—or the freedom—to take risks earlier on. Or they may need to work in a traditional job first in order to gain the skills they'll later need to run a business or to realize they aren't cut out for a traditional job. That's what happened to Diana Olsen, who graduated from university with a degree in French literature, an aesthete's eye for beauty, and an appreciation of all things organic—a combination that fed her soul but qualified her to work in, yes, a cubicle providing customer service for a large automobile company. Stifled and restless, she started dreading Monday morning—on Friday night. "I knew I had more to offer," she explains. "I couldn't just do or be one piece of a machine. My mind wants me to operate the entire machine and think about creating things and problem-solving on a bigger level."

Diana needed to work for someone else to realize she'd never be happy working for anyone but herself. But the job—her last gig as an employee—wasn't a complete waste of her time or talent. On her lunch breaks, she came up with the idea for Balzac's Coffee: European-style cafés serving hand-crafted coffee with an emphasis on all things organic, sustainable, and local. The antithesis of Starbucks, in other words. "I drew out a plan for the first café on my breaks," Diana remembers. "I still have my little scratch pad." The first Balzac's opened in 1996, and now there are eight in southern Ontario, two of which my fellow dragon Bruce Croxon and I helped fund after we partnered with Diana in Balzac's following her successful 2011 *Dragons' Den* pitch.

Sometimes, the decision to leap to an entrepreneurial lifestyle is a reaction not to a current job but to a major shift in life circumstances. That was the case with me. Unlike many entrepreneurs, I didn't grow up believing I was destined to run a business. I discovered my calling at 31, after I got divorced and my whole world turned upside down. I had four kids, a high school diploma, and a bitter custody battle on my hands. I needed money, fast, and the opportunity to get in on the ground level of a start-up and earn equity seemed like my best shot. Turned out it was.

Many entrepreneurs have similar stories: a significant setback prompted a major life change. Sometimes, an early loss or trauma is the fire in which the entrepreneur is forged. Take Greg Chamandy, the co-founder of Gildan Activewear, whose father died when Greg was just five. That loss gave Greg a sense that life was short and he'd better get going if he wanted to make his mark. As a kid, he spent weekends working in the shipping room of his grandfather's garment factory; as a teenager, he often spent his spring break on the road with the company salesman. At 18, when many of his friends went off to university, he joined the family business full-time. (Early hardship also played a pivotal role in turning my friend Annette Verschuren, executive chairwoman of NRStor Inc., into a successful entrepreneur—but more on her story later.)

For Wayne Fromm, the motivating factor was his father's death in a car accident on the day after Father's Day at the age of 60. Wayne, who was 34 at the time, was busy with Video Invasion, the coin-operated family entertainment centres he'd created. But the tragedy brought clarity and focus. Suddenly aware of how life can change in an instant, he decided it was high time to pursue his dream of becoming an inventor. What was he waiting for? Wayne began to create toys—the first, a bubble pendant for kids to wear—and got his start by cold-calling the Walt Disney Company and wangling a meeting. (He ended up transforming the pendant into a Little Mermaid item for Disney.) Today, he's a successful toy inventor and entrepreneur, responsible for creating everything from talking mirrors to milkshake makers.

There's no single tried-and-true route to entrepreneurship.

And there's no age limit, either. The door never slams shut, though there are certain advantages (and disadvantages) at every stage of life. At 25, you may lack capital and experience, but in terms of having the emotional wherewithal and physical stamina to withstand the stress and punishing hours, you may have a real advantage. At 45, you may be saddled with baggage— mortgages, children, possibly a limiting CV—but you have the wisdom that comes from experience and the rejuvenating jolt of determination that accompanies a desire for personal reinvention. At 60, you may have entirely different motivations: perhaps you've been downsized from a corporate job but can't afford to retire, or maybe retirement scares you almost as much as mortality. On the plus side, you've probably already forged a secure sense of your own identity and abilities, and, because of that, may have more confidence and a greater appetite for risk than ever before.

The key isn't when you were born but whether you want independence enough, by which I mean so much so that you're willing to tolerate discomfort. You also have to be ready to make decisions with imperfect information, and you need the emotional resources to sustain yourself when no one around you seems to believe in you or your vision. That isn't something you can learn or I can teach. You either have it, because you're compelled by the need to run your own show (and you have the emotional self-sufficiency required to do so), or you don't.

The conviction I'm talking about here is very similar to the kind you see in an athlete who was born to race. If you were born to run, you have to run. You just won't be able to stop yourself. Recently, I watched a documentary about young girls in a small Ethiopian community that's produced a disproportionately large number of the world's top marathon runners. The community's entire economy is based on selecting the best runners, teaching them how to race, and then sending them off to perform on the world stage. When you watch these girls, you can tell right away which ones have no doubt that running is their calling. Their ability is innate, but the skill and endurance are something they've honed over time.

The same is true of entrepreneurs. Just as a born runner starts to feel stiff and restless when she isn't running, entrepreneurs feel caged in when they can't run with their ideas, or transform their dreams into something tangible and real. When you're a born entrepreneur, you never really feel fulfilled when you're building someone else's plan. There's something in you that needs to strike out on your own. You crave independence, freedom, and wide-open spaces.

Chapter 2

Core Strengths

True independence—*and being happy being independent*—
requires anticipating and coping with a unique set of psychological and emotional challenges. Autonomy, particularly the
type entrepreneurs must embrace, calls for mental toughness,
self-discipline, and self-reliance. Carving out an independent path takes courage, focus, and emotional resilience, the sort
where setbacks don't faze you and criticism doesn't upset you. A
touch of monomaniacal self-assurance, seasoned with a dash of
self-doubt, doesn't hurt, either. You need to be able and willing
to be your own coach and cheerleader, so you can talk yourself
back on track and spur yourself on after a failure. And you need
to be able to do all this while others are rolling their eyes and tut-
tutting about your "impossible dreams" and "crazy ideas." (Get
ready: with independence come naysayers, sometimes truckloads
of them.)

So how do you develop and maintain these core emotional
strengths? For starters, you recognize that they're essential

ingredients of the entrepreneurial lifestyle. You simply will not enjoy this life if you lack them. You need to build yourself up emotionally in much the same way that you exercise and develop different muscle groups at the gym, and for much the same reason: so you get stronger, and so you don't wind up sidelined by preventable injuries. The point isn't to approach being an entrepreneur as facing a painful set of chores you have to suffer through. The point is to love it (even on the days when you hate it) and to be good at it. And your chances of doing so are far, far better if you're conscious of the need for emotional resilience and continually working to strengthen it.

Everyone knows that you can't start a business without some grasp of the laws of supply and demand. Few people stop to think about the laws of emotional supply and demand, but knowing what they are is equally if not even more important. The issue, for anyone who's truly independent, is that you control *both* supply and demand.

Stoking the Fire in Your Belly

When you're the boss of your own life, feeling motivated is not generally a problem. This is especially true if you've left the corporate world and are starting over, on your own. In the beginning, everything is new and shiny with possibility. You may feel daunted by the challenge, but you also feel energized. Because entrepreneurs love what we do, and because there's always so much to do, we rarely wake up with that "Oh, God, it's Monday morning" feeling. Often, business is the first thing we think about in the morning and the last thing we think about at night—and we're happy with this arrangement. In fact, sometimes we're so motivated that we seem obsessed. Forcing yourself to focus on work isn't the problem. It's prying yourself loose so you remember to send flowers on Mother's Day or your anniversary.

Being an entrepreneur is a lot like being in love: you're totally into your work and want to spend every waking second with it. However, as anyone who's ever been in love knows, at some point the honeymoon is over. And as any marriage counsellor will tell you, that's when the hard work of a successful marriage begins.

It's important to know from the start that as much as you love what you do, and as fulfilled as you feel by it, at some point the honeymoon *will* be over. Count on having days when you feel that nothing is moving forward and you're stuck in quicksand. Count on fearing that you've made a terrible mistake.

Take Peter Neal, for instance, who runs a successful specialty food distribution company, Neal Brothers Foods, with his older brother Chris. Today, the company has carved out a profitable niche distributing natural and specialty foods to stores. Despite the company's success, Peter still has vivid memories of its painful growth phase, when he sometimes questioned whether the decision to strike out as an entrepreneur was a grave mistake. The stress left "a taste that's never far from my mouth."

He and his brother were on summer break from university when they started making croutons in their family's kitchen and selling them in local markets. Six weeks after they made their first batch, Peter came home at the end of the day to find his parents' answering machine filled with messages from stores requesting more croutons because they had sold out. "We had some success quickly and thought we had a really great business," remembers Peter. It took about 18 months for their initial high to wear off, but when it finally did, the Neal brothers faced many, many tough years.

While their friends dated, took holidays, and backpacked around Europe, Peter and Chris were pulling all-nighters baking bread. "We'd often work 20-hour days and take turns sleeping on bags of flour on the floor."

By day, the brothers travelled from one grocery store to another, stocking shelves and doing product demonstrations, or writing proposals to try to get their products into new chains or specialty markets. While they were prepared that the entrepreneurial journey would be tough, they didn't realize just how long their money-less streak would last. Five years after starting the company, Peter proposed to his girlfriend with a $1,500 ring he'd bought from Birks on a three-part payment plan—only he wasn't able to make the final payment, which meant he was saddled with a poor credit rating for years. "I couldn't even afford an extra $500," says Peter, who was living rent-free at his parents' place at the time.

Far harder than being broke, however, was the shame they felt after years of grunt work with little to show for their labours. Peter remembers doing a product demo with his brother at Pusateri's, a large specialty foods retailer in Toronto. They were wearing aprons and handing out food samples. One shopper approached and told them the croutons were good, but it was a "shame that grown boys like you are demo-ing food." A couple of months later, after the brothers had expanded into specialty food distribution, Peter was on his hands and knees, stocking shelves in a store in downtown Toronto, when an old friend from university—now a banker—approached him and asked how his "little crouton company" was going. "He was making hundreds of thousands of dollars on Bay Street. I was on my hands and knees scraping by on eight grand a year. I remember thinking, 'Oh, my God, could I get any lower?'"

Most entrepreneurs I know have similar horror stories about the excruciating shame we feel when the initial burst of passion has faded but our businesses have yet to turn a profit. These feelings are completely normal and not an indication that you have no business running your own business. Every entrepreneur has days that include doubt and uncertainty. But because you're in control and therefore flying solo—even if you have employees— niggling questions and doubts can snowball into the-sky-is-falling, catastrophic anxiety. I remember moments when I thought, *If I'm questioning this venture, what are other people saying? I'm doomed.* And because what you're doing is an extension of your personality and the ultimate test of your abilities, as doubts multiply, they start to eat away at your self-confidence. If that vicious cycle begins, your motivation will almost certainly flag.

These bouts of anxiety aren't simply for rookies, either. Experienced entrepreneurs battle them every day. When I invest in or acquire a new company, I always wrestle with the challenges that come with any new start-up. There are days when my fears that I have made an unwise decision are overwhelming.

But when you're independent, you no longer have the luxury of dialling it in at work for a few days while you mentally regroup. When time is money—yours, the bank's, and/or your friends' and family's—you don't have the option of slipping into idle. You have to find a way to conquer your demons, or at least get them to shut up, and carry on. Immediately.

One of the best ways to do this is to acknowledge from the outset that bad days and self-doubts are part of the price of independence. I don't know a single entrepreneur who hasn't had to foot that particular bill. In retrospect, a surprising number are even happy they paid it. Many of the entrepreneurs I interviewed for this book spoke of feeling like "frauds" early on. The "fraud syndrome" is something I've encountered a lot in my work as a marketer, especially with entrepreneurs. Often when I sit down with an entrepreneur and ask him to tell me about his business, I'll get answers delivered in that same apologetic tone I used when I described my company at that Calgary dinner party. Because I've been there, I understand where the inner conflict is coming from. We live in a world which demands that leaders have all the answers, all the time. But the entrepreneur is charting a path whose road he can't possibly visualize. And it's this uncertainty—not the feeling that he is incapable—that's at the heart of the imposter syndrome. The interesting thing is that, again and again, these same so-called imposter syndrome sufferers told me that their uncertainty and insecurity actually drove them to accomplish amazing things.

Second, you need a bulletproof reason to keep going no matter how uncertain or daunted you feel. It can help to write it down on a piece of paper. On the days when you pull it out of your pocket to remind yourself why you've chosen a course that may seem suddenly borderline insane, your raison d'être needs to answer every question and defuse every doubt.

When I started out in the business world, I had the most bulletproof reason imaginable: I wanted custody of my kids. After my divorce, a family court judge told me that if I wanted my children to live with me full-time, I had to prove that I could provide for them. At the time I was sleeping on my dad's couch, crying a lot, and wondering what was to become of me. My sole credential was a high school diploma. I'll be forever grateful to my dad for pulling me out of my pity party, because I was so devastated I'm not sure I would have had the strength to do it as quickly without him. I can remember Dad coming in and finding me on the couch (a post I hadn't vacated in weeks), drowning in my tears. "You've got to get up off your ass and do something," he told me, "because if you don't do it, no one is going to do it for you." Looking back I see that while my dad thought he was giving me advice on how to regain custody of my kids, he was also giving me the best message you could ever give an entrepreneur: the buck stops with you. So you can't stop—no matter what.

Naturally, when the going got really tough, the flame sputtered a bit. However, on days when I felt depleted or inadequate, that goal—getting my kids back—kept me going. It helped a lot that I felt I had no choice in the matter: I simply wasn't willing to entertain the possibility that my children and I might never again live under the same roof. While I certainly had concerns and doubts about whether my business would succeed, clarity of purpose gave me the strength to deal with them and helped ensure that my fears didn't topple me or my business. In my experience, fear can be an excellent motivator. The trick is to make it your friend instead of your enemy and find a way to harness its galvanizing power, not be paralyzed by it.

You need your own bulletproof reason for doing what you're doing, and it helps to articulate it clearly to yourself. A vague mission statement like "I want to make some money for a change" just won't cut it when you're having a dark night of the soul and questioning why you're bothering with this idiotic business, anyway. Peter Neal attached a piece of paper to the sun visor in his car that read, "I promise my brother, my wife, and myself that I'm going to make a million dollars in sales." His mantra reinforced his dream and gave him a crystal clear goal to work toward on days when he felt like quitting. A friend who's worked for herself all her life told me what keeps her going is her conviction that when she turns 50, she's going to live on an island year-round. A photo of a pristine beach hangs over her desk to serve as a touchstone when she feels like throwing in the towel. Another entrepreneur I know looks backward, not forward, for motivation: his bulletproof reason is that he wants to "show" those kids who tormented him in high school. To me, this motivation seems crazy; the guy is a multi-millionaire—get over it, already. But it works for him, and that's all your own reason needs to do: restart your engines when they threaten to stall.

Another strategy that works well when doubt starts gnawing at the edges of your resolve is to tell yourself that as bad as things are, they could always be worse. For some entrepreneurs, worse may mean working for somebody else. Everybody's worst-case scenario differs, but sometimes simply forcing yourself to con-template the prospect of having to get "a real job" or return to the corporate world again does the trick nicely. Early on, the idea of working for someone else—and possibly enduring the humiliation of getting fired (again) because I didn't "fit"—was the only worst-case scenario I needed. Today, my fears over los-ing custody of my children are long behind me and my bullet-proof reason has changed. What drives me now is my passion for entrepreneurship plus the inner voice urging me to use my experiences, network, and influence to help other entrepreneurs succeed. Responding to this calling is my bulletproof reason. The idea of having to ignore that powerful inner voice is my worst-case scenario.

No matter how apprehensive or overwhelmed you may feel at a given moment, the idea of having to relinquish your hard-won independence can be even more terrifying. Sometimes thinking about your worst-case scenario will provide the jolt of adrenaline you need to get yourself back on track. One young entrepreneur I know of went one step further: on days when the doldrums hit, she'd go visit friends who still worked for other people. They were perfectly happy in their jobs. But for her, the mere sight of a cubicle served as a bracing reminder of why she'd sought—and wouldn't dream of surrendering—the creative freedom of being an independent entrepreneur.

Mastering the Three Rs: Roadblocks, Rejection, Resilience

To some people, obstacles and barriers seem insurmountable. They run out of steam when they encounter one hurdle after another and start daydreaming about an easier, 9 to 5 existence. Entrepreneurs who are intent on doing things their way, however, will often tell you (okay, after the fact, when the pain is a distant memory) that obstacles *helped* motivate them. I'm one of those annoying people, but I think it's true: obstacles are just challenges to be overcome or detoured around.

If you crave independence, you likely share this mindset. You're so intent on doing things your way that probably you're already inclined to view problems as solvable. But even if that's not your natural instinct, I think it's possible to train yourself to reframe problems positively, as challenges. It all comes down to learning to monitor your reactions—both mental and emotional—when there's a challenge. If you tend to absorb the negative, take it onboard, and promptly start wilting, you'll need to make a conscious effort to cultivate your inner resilience.

I had to, too. When I first ran my own business, people often said to me, "Why would we lend *you* money?" The first few times

I slunk off apologetically, feeling small. But I quickly realized that if I didn't react differently, I was actually proving them right. So I trained myself to ignore my instincts and, whenever the gauntlet was thrown down, stood my ground and tried to persuade banks and other lenders that there were actually quite a few good reasons to loan me—unproven, but ambitious and focused me—money. Surprisingly often, simply by calmly making my case in a way that acknowledged the risks but also the potential rewards to investors, I was able to make my case. I think they saw something in me that I didn't see in myself.

In the process, I learned to think differently about roadblocks. In business, so long as your manner is not obnoxious or cocky it is quite possible to convert an initial "no" to a "yes." It happens all the time, in fact—so long as you don't walk away at the first sign of resistance, respond emotionally, or sit down in front of the barrier and give up. That knowledge made me much more resilient and persistent in business.

Most entrepreneurs' responses to roadblocks and rejection have been forged in a similar sort of fire. Take 27-year-old Natasha Vandenhurk, for instance, who's director of sales and marketing at Canpressco Products Inc., which is the home of Three Farmers Camelina Oil. In 2009, Natasha's dad, a Saskatchewan farmer, became excited about camelina seed, a nutritionally rich crop that grows extremely well in the prairies and, as he and his partners discovered, can be cold-pressed into a cooking oil. At the time, all they'd done was crush and test a few batches of oil and submit an application for Health Canada's approval. They hadn't heard back from the government yet, nor did they have any clue about strategy, branding, or how to get their product to market. Natasha's dad wanted to know if she had any interest in taking the reins and launching their product.

Natasha had just earned a degree in economics and was working at an estate-planning firm. She had never run a company but always dreamed of doing so and leaped at the chance. Still, as exciting as she found the prospect, she also found it "super-intimidating." Once she plunged in, it felt even more intimidating: she had to prove herself not just once or twice, but over and over again. And she had to do it knowing if she failed, she'd be letting down not only herself, but also everyone who'd sunk money into the company, like her father, neighbours, and family friends she'd known her entire life. Natasha was, in her words, "plagued with self-doubt every day." She also knew that, unchecked, her self-doubt would make her indecisive and ineffective. It might even finish off the business.

First, she had to develop a thicker skin so she could handle rejection and move on emotionally, instead of concluding that whoever was rejecting her knew more than she did and therefore must be right. Early on, Natasha's former boss set her up with two "marketing gurus" for advice on bringing her product to market. She was excited: expert help! On a conference call, she eagerly told them about the oil's properties, sent them some samples, and waited not so patiently for their words of wisdom. Two weeks later, the phone finally rang and the pearls of advice were finally delivered. "They said we didn't have anything and I should really rethink what I was doing with my life and where I was going with my career," Natasha remembers. She hung up and proceeded to weep in her office for two hours. Today, she looks back on that phone call with something close to affection.

The negative feedback, she says, wound up fuelling her determination. "I thought, 'I have to *do* something. I'm going to make something of this.'"

But things didn't turn on a dime, either with the business or with her self-belief. Not long afterward, having exhaustively researched branding and packaging options, solicited quotes from various agencies, and even located a funding organization willing to underwrite 50 percent of the branding costs, she met with investors to present her conclusions. She was convinced she'd found the best way to begin marketing the oil to specialty retailers and independents. One shareholder, however, thought that branding and packaging were frills. He felt spending time and money on such things would be a waste—surely Natasha's top priority should be getting the product out there ASAP? The other investors didn't see why she couldn't simply handle the branding and packaging in-house. Why get fancy firms involved?

For Natasha, who was then 24 and had approached the meeting with the kind of buoyancy that comes from knowing you've wrestled a tough problem and finally hit on the right answer, being told no was completely flattening. In fact, she burst into tears. "I was mortified," she remembers today. "How unprofessional is that? They put me in charge, and here I am bawling in a meeting!"

But after reflecting on why and how the meeting went wrong and talking things over with her father, she was able to get some perspective on the situation. Yes, she was facing a serious roadblock, but perhaps she'd actually helped construct it. Which meant that maybe she could tear it down, too.

She realized that maybe she hadn't done the best job of communicating how she'd arrived at her decisions. Perhaps she hadn't made it clear to the investors that her conclusions were backed by considerable research and analysis. She wanted a redo, but to get one she first had to show them that she'd heard them—and there was a good reason for them to listen to her, too. So she followed the shareholders' instructions and, in collaboration with an IT guy who worked for one of the investors, gamely tried to spruce up Canpressco's old website. Neither of them was a designer, though, so the result was pretty terrible. She didn't set out to create a bad website—quite the opposite—but now she had concrete evidence to support her argument that the design work should be outsourced. Eventually she got the green light.

Along the way, she learned something important: being young doesn't mean your judgment is terrible. Natasha's instincts were good and her research was sound. What she needed to work on was communicating authoritatively and comprehensively with shareholders—and one thing she needed to communicate was calm self-confidence. When your response to rejection is emotional, as though it's you personally rather than your idea that's being rejected, you can pretty much count on roadblocks. This result is especially true when, like Natasha, you haven't had a chance to prove yourself yet. Others can't look to your track record for assurance, and you haven't yet developed enough confidence to calmly assuage their concerns. One way to eliminate roadblocks, she realized, was to stop helping create them by asking for approval from shareholders on every decision. So, having tried things the investors' way, she firmly told them that micromanaging her was not going to work. If they were going to trust her to run the company, they had to trust her judgment, too. Going forward, they did.

Hearing "no" over and over can be soul-destroying. Or it can be the making of you, as it was for Natasha, who traces her resilience and conviction directly to learning how to process rejection.

She explains, "I've become numb to the word 'no.' I'm not going to stop just because somebody doesn't understand the market or the product. At the same time, I have to be open to criticism and feedback, because maybe there's some merit in it. That's why self-doubt is such a dangerous thing. You have to take that criticism, pick it apart, and find the value of it, without letting it fuel your self-doubt. You have to tell yourself, 'I have to find a way to make this work.'"

As an entrepreneur, you need to develop radar for—and a defence system to protect you from—the naysayers. If you're already feeling vulnerable or uneasy, their negativity can severely undermine your confidence. But as Natasha points out, you can't disregard naysayers altogether. There may be a kernel of truth in what they're saying, so you have to dissect their observations, quickly and clinically, to try to find it.

Part of the learning curve is developing a knack for distinguishing between people who are offering—or at least genuinely believe they're offering—constructive criticism and those who view naysaying as a form of entertainment or blood sport. Entrepreneurs, I've found, seem to attract more than their fair share of the latter. Departing from the conventional path to do something risky—especially when what you're doing is pursuing a dream—may alarm or offend others. Maybe they view your choices as a rejection of their own choices in life. Perhaps they feel threatened precisely because they long to take a similar sort of risk themselves, but don't have the stomach for it. Whatever the case, naysayers of this ilk are hazardous to your emotional health and you need to distance yourself, emotionally, to defuse the power of their words.

Sometimes, though, people aren't aiming to make you feel bad. They just don't understand the choices you've made, which is why they're questioning them. I heard this from Brad Rabiey who, along with his wife, Rebecca, launched The Carbon Farmer on the Rabiey family farm in Alberta. The idea behind their company is this: individuals and corporations wishing to offset their carbon footprint pay the Rabieys to plant trees. Before launching their pilot project in 2007, Brad worked in various government jobs. (Rebecca was—and remains—a full-time social worker, but The Carbon Farmer is very much a partnership.) All the time, Brad says, he encounters people who just don't know what to make of the life he's chosen. "Why leave a safe, well-paying job with fantastic benefits and security?"

Brad has come to believe there are two types of people. Some see their careers as a means to an end: they go to work and limit their hours as much as possible so they have time to do the things they really want to do. But for others, work is the whole point: they do what they love and try to find a way to get paid for it. Those in the first group, Brad explains, complain when they have to put in a couple of hours of overtime at work. So when they see someone who barely has time to socialize or participate in recreational activities anymore, especially someone with an unconventional business model, they can't comprehend what could possibly be driving him to work so hard. Entrepreneurs, as well as farmers, are in the second category: our work is our life.

Brad tries to explain by saying, "Nobody is forcing me to do this. It's my own choice and I'm loving every minute of it. So I don't mind working late or forgoing leisure activities. I wake up every morning excited for the day to begin." But, he says, people who work to live just don't seem to get the idea of living to work. It's helpful to bear this attitude in mind when you encounter a naysayer: maybe the person isn't sneering at you or your business idea. Maybe their way of life and values are just so different that they don't have a frame of reference for understanding yours.

Cultivating a Zen Outlook (Though You're Really a Type A)

When you're an entrepreneur, you carry the entire burden of responsibility for the success or failure of your enterprise. So when a crisis erupts, everyone, including you, will be looking to you for cues on how to respond. If you're feeling attacked—by investors, say, or by distributors who seem intent on wrecking your business—your first impulse may be to flip out or lash out. If you've contributed to the crisis or perhaps even directly caused it, retreating to a corner to berate yourself may seem like a fine idea. As tempting as that may be, however, you're going to need a more effective long-term strategy.

The truth is that you're going to face crises, and at least some of them will be your fault. You're going to make mistakes. All entrepreneurs do. The challenge is how to respond to them.

In a recent speech at his alma mater, Ridley College, my fellow dragon, Lavalife co-founder Bruce Croxon, described what he calls a 51/49 rule. He said that when he looks back on his career, he can see that he's had victories 51 percent of the time and defeats 49 percent of the time. While he believes that that 2 percent margin creates enough leeway for a successful career, he says that what truly matters is how you live with the 49 percent—the mistakes and losses. If you're the kind of person who radiates feelings of failure—you come home after a bad day and slam doors, or snap at your spouse, or lie awake all night fretting and worrying—then the entrepreneurial lifestyle is not for you (or for anyone who has to live with you).

Learning to cultivate a Zen outlook is paramount, and that can be particularly different for independent types because we're control freaks by nature. We don't want to go with the flow of traffic; we want to direct it. So being philosophical when things go wrong isn't our first instinct. But when all hell is breaking loose, by far the best response is to focus, consciously, on keeping your head and trusting that the universe will unfold as it should. A tall order for anyone who's Type A, to be sure. But here's why I think it's possible: most of us already *are* responding this way in other areas of our lives. Even the most controlling entrepreneur has the capacity to take a deep breath and look at the big picture.

My Zen outlook was put to the test during the major floods that hit Calgary in the summer of 2013. Heavy rains caused the Bow River to break its banks and pour water into the city. Much of the downtown core remained underwater for more than a week, including Venture's offices. My staff was forced to work remotely from dozens of different locations across the city. Our Toronto office stepped in and helped save the day by assisting with the workload, but our ability to deliver on promises made to clients was severely challenged. And while our clients were extremely supportive, I knew that I had a limited time frame in which to find a solution that would bring a state of normalcy back to the company.

Meanwhile, I was still dealing with the start-up challenges associated with YouInc, overseeing my other investments, working on this book, and taping new segments for *Dragons' Den* and *The Big Decision.* None of the other commitments let up. For more than a week, I felt my stress level rising. I was snappish with my team and my family, and had a hard time sleeping, making me even more irritable. On the day I was booked to view some new office space with a real estate agent, I barked at my assistant and sent her a harshly worded email. I called for a cab to take me to the new loca-tion, but was put on hold for so long I thought I'd have better luck trying to hail one from the sidewalk. I walked for blocks without finding a taxi. The Stampede was on and the downtown was packed with people—most of whom also seemed to need a taxi. At some point, I realized I was so late that I had missed the window to view the building I most wanted to rent. My already high stress levels surged even higher. I felt a crushing weight on my shoulders that made it hard to breathe.

Fifteen years ago, I would not have been able to view my situa-tion philosophically and resolve it. But years of training myself to cultivate a Zen outlook have paid off. I reminded myself that all the panic in the world wouldn't get me a taxi. I took some slow, deep breaths. I focused on happy thoughts (for me, the happiest thing to think about is always my grandchildren). Every time my mind tried to go back to the panic of work, and being harsh with my assistant, and how we could possibly handle moving offices with all the work on our plates, I took another deep breath and asked myself what my grandchildren were doing at this very moment. Within minutes my panic subsided and I was able to think clearly again.

Distinguishing Between Big Problems and Little Problems

When you raise kids, you learn pretty quickly to distinguish between a problem that requires a bandage and a reassuring hug, and one that requires a trip to the emergency room. Being a parent teaches you to be decisive rather than dithering. It also teaches you how to triage. Both abilities have served me well as an entrepreneur. Sometimes, I consciously try to revert to parental mode when there's a real problem at work. First, I decide whether it truly qualifies as a crisis or if it's just a lot of noise surrounding the event. If it really is a crisis, I spring into first-responder mode, just as I did when my kids were little. But once I've done what I can, I consider the problem to be in the hands of the gods and refocus my energy on other matters. If the problem is so stressful that it causes me to start playing out worst-case scenarios in my head, I have trained myself to turn that particular movie reel off (just as I did, by the way, when my kids were teenagers and out late at night). I don't think of what I'm doing as denial. I think of it as self-preservation.

When you're an entrepreneur dealing with a crisis, whether it's immediate or long-term, nothing is more important than perspective. You can't do without it if you're going to play the long game. Sometimes I regain my perspective simply by distracting myself, maybe via a glass of wine and a good book, or by taking a break to connect with my family and friends. But one of the best ways I have found is to look for perspective beyond my own office. I devote a lot of time to charities for disadvantaged kids because it's an issue I care about deeply, but there's self-interest at work, too. Helping kids who have so little—not even something to eat for breakfast, in many homes in Canada—is one of the fastest ways to bring myself back to earth and stay grounded.

Looking at my business problems through that lens helps me realize how trivial most of them really are. If I allow myself to wallow, worrying and constantly forecasting doom, it's just a huge waste of time. Survival depends on developing strategies for managing worry. Personally, I'm strict with myself because worry is completely useless. It solves nothing and actually promotes dysfunction. Allow worry to proceed unchecked and it can turn into a soul-sucking monster that will voraciously consume your emotional capital—capital you should be investing in promoting the success of your business, not fretting about its failure.

One of the most insidious aspects of worrying is that it can fool you into thinking that wringing your hands is the same as doing something to solve your problem. It can function as an unconscious form of busy work, or as a penance you inflict on yourself for not addressing your problem more directly.

Remember my worries about making the right decisions for YouInc, the technology company I'm building? Very often those worries begin as a legitimate form of troubleshooting: "Is this person the right individual to help me build my team, or should I hire that other person?" "Am I working with the right programmer, or do I need someone with a totally different set of skills?" If left unchecked, this kind of second-guessing can spiral into crippling self-doubt. I start to ask myself if I was crazy to get into this new business. I wonder if I'm smart enough to pull it off—again.

I've learned to recognize when I'm hurtling into the dangerous territory of self-doubt and solo-worry. As soon as I catch myself doing it, I'll call in the reserves—usually an entrepreneur I trust who has some expertise in the area I'm worrying about. That's exactly what I did a few months ago when I was in a full-on panic about my new business. I talked through my concerns and found that just hearing myself express my worries was enough to deflate most of the anxiety I'd been feeling. That night I slept soundly for the first time in weeks. Did I solve all the problems? No. But I lowered my anxiety level enough to begin thinking them through logically.

Just as I have learned to become mindful about the foods I

eat, I've also trained myself to be mindful when I'm worrying. So I recognize what I'm doing, consciously switch it off, and try to focus on something else. All entrepreneurs need to be able to do this. If you can't, the uncertainty and problems that come with any independent venture will drive you around the bend.

Learning to Embrace the Mess

A good litmus test for deciding whether you're cut out for independence is to ask yourself whether you can live comfortably with a certain amount of mess. It's an important question—maybe one of the most crucial for you to consider—because mess comes with the territory. So does ambiguity. If a lack of predictability makes you crazy, and if you can't relax until every loose end is tied up neatly, independence will reduce you to a nervous wreck.

Running your own business, you never feel you've taken care of everything and can just kick back and coast. You never feel you have all the answers—or even all the questions. Even after you've been an entrepreneur for decades, you're still figuring things out as you go. And that's part of the joy of it, frankly: the feeling that every day brings something new, and who knows what might happen next?

You'll have a much easier time adjusting to the lifestyle, and you'll certainly be a whole lot happier, if you're naturally inclined to manage on the fly and readjust when necessary rather than insisting that you have to stick with Plan A. Being comfortable with improvisation really, really helps. Successful entrepreneurs are masters at tapping into whatever resources are on hand, according to one study I read recently, "What Makes Entrepreneurs Entrepreneurial?" by University of Virginia professor Saras D.

Sarasvathy. In the study, Dr. Sarasvathy compares entrepreneurs to Iron Chefs—those wizards capable of throwing together whatever mundane or exotic ingredients are available to create something surprising and delicious. Corporate leaders, by contrast, set out with specific goals in mind and work toward achieving them in a linear, efficient, cost-effective manner.

Improvisation is so much a part of the daily life of an entrepreneur that we may as well be stand-up comics. Stand-ups spend a lot of time alone crafting their material, but at a certain point they have to take their act on the road and test it in front of an audience. Performing is the only way to perfect their timing and find out where the laughs are. To some degree, every performance is a walk on the wild side, but once they master their material and get some experience handling hecklers, they're not in total freefall. They also start to feed off the adrenaline rush that comes from performing and helps them improvise even better lines and comebacks. It's the same for entrepreneurs: you need to prepare like crazy, but then at a certain point, you also need to loosen up and expect the unexpected—and start to enjoy the unexpectedness.

If you're the sort of person who prefers life to unfold in a linear and predictable fashion, you're also going to need to train yourself to cope with unpredictability. One good way is simply to force yourself into situations where you will have no choice but to improvise: try your hand at stand-up comedy, for instance, to develop confidence in your own quick-wittedness and ability to think on your feet. That's what Spanx founder and billionaire Sara Blakely did. She told *Forbes* that she performed amateur stand-up at night while she was trying to build her company. It didn't come easily. In fact, every time she went onstage, she says, she almost threw up. "I learned why they called it the green room," she once quipped. And yet she forced herself to confront her fears and need for predictability rather than be constrained by them. She learned that she could, in fact, improvise under pressure. She might never love doing it, but she was able to pull it off.

There's no confidence like the confidence that comes from having confronted something you feared. Pushing yourself beyond your own comfort zone is probably the most effective strategy for growth and the development of new talents, both personally and professionally. Fear is related to not knowing what to expect and not being sure you can deliver it; it's connected to the mess and ambiguity that go along with unpredictability. You can be the most independent person in the world, and the most talented at improv, yet still have that fear. The only way I've ever learned to overcome it is simply to do whatever the thing is that makes me afraid.

For me, one of these things was appearing on a TV show. The idea of people studying my flaws in high definition and dissecting my logic with the help of a rewind button scared me half to death. Worse, I didn't know whether it would be worth it. What if I went through the humiliation of exposing myself and, in the end, there was no reward? Not knowing how things would turn out was a huge disincentive. I went ahead anyway and discovered that I enjoyed the opportunity. Being on *Dragons' Den* and *The Big Decision* has helped me grow as a person—and helped my business grow, too. If I'd paid closer attention to my fears, my life simply would not be as rich today. I'm not talking about money, by the way, but about the enjoyment and tremendous range of experiences and opportunities that have opened up to me as a result. My work on television was instrumental in helping me uncover a new passion: helping other entrepreneurs. If I hadn't confronted my fear of going on TV, I might have never launched YouInc or written two books.

As an entrepreneur, you're going to be facing your fears daily. Often, that's because the best opportunities for growth lie far beyond terra cognita—familiar territory. Take body language expert Mark Bowden, for example. When it comes to understanding non-verbal communication, Mark is undoubtedly an expert. But as a consultant to international business leaders and political honchos, he has to confront unknown and often high-pressure situations every day.

In the 1990s, Mark was a successful actor and theatre producer in Europe and considered a pioneer in "physical theatre"—a form of acting that emphasizes physical movement over speech. In 2000, after a large UK-based firm paid him the equivalent of about a month's acting salary to help train its managers in communication techniques, he discovered an opportunity to use his acting expertise in a totally new environment—the corporate world.

For the next five years, he picked up training contracts in between acting gigs. But in 2005, when he decided to quit acting and move his family to Toronto for good, TRUTHPLANE was born. Within months, Mark was training senior corporate and political leaders in the art of effective non-verbal communication. And while the nature of his training doesn't change from one client to the next, the environment he needs to adapt to evolves constantly—which is both stressful and fear-inducing. For instance, Mark was recently invited to give a lecture on non-verbal communication to an international conference of brain surgeons. "Here I was, about to talk to neurosurgeons about neurobiology and neuro-architecture. I thought, 'Surely someone's going to call me out.'" A part of him was completely terrified. "I knew I was an expert in my field, and I believed I could deliver. Yet part of me felt like an imposter in their world." But he'd already signed the contract, boarded the plane, and cashed the cheque. Hundreds of neurosurgeons awaited him in the audience. Failure just wasn't an option. He breathed deeply and summoned his years of acting experience to help him confront his fear and deliver one of his best talks ever.

Mark's story illustrates a great point about fear—it never goes away for entrepreneurs. Ever. That's because challenging the status quo and embracing the unknown is our modus operandi. Facing his fears that day at the neuroscience conference hasn't helped Mark assuage them over the long haul—fear is as much a part of his internal landscape today as it was years ago. But the way he views it is different. "I understand that it's just a part of the game; it's something I have to manage." When he faces the old "imposter" fears today, he makes a mental distinction about what specifically it is that he's afraid of. "I remind myself I'm not an imposter in the skills and experience I have. I'm simply entering a world I may never have been in before."

Unfortunately, there isn't any magic formula for cultivating an appetite for chaos. You simply can't know, going in, how everything will turn out. And the beginning, middle, and end of the story may never be entirely clear. But a little messiness isn't going to kill you. Especially if you understand it's a normal aspect of the entrepreneurial life.

Recognizing Your Strengths—and Recruiting to Compensate for Your Weaknesses

You work independently as an entrepreneur, but chances are extremely good that your long-term survival will depend on drawing on the skills and talents of others to complement your limitations. First, though, you need to diagnose what your strengths and weaknesses actually are. If you're an escapee from the corporate world, you've also escaped the annual performance review, which is why it's so important to engage in some disciplined self-reflection from time to time. But that can be a problem if you're one of those entrepreneurs with an outsized ego, because the supreme self-confidence that enables you to take on difficult challenges may also blind you to your flaws and failings. So it's important to ask yourself some tough questions, as well as to ask for and listen to hard-nosed assessments from people you trust and respect, even though what they're telling you may be hard to hear.

Do your exceptionally high standards make you too harsh a judge of yourself and others, even when they stumble over something small? Is your passion the engine that drives you, but also a flaw because it clouds your judgment? Are you legendarily determined, but a terrible listener inclined to believe that you're infallible? I see examples of these traits all the time on *Dragons' Den*: entrepreneurs who are so blinded by their passion that they are unwilling to accept valuable feedback from a panel of experienced entrepreneurs and investors.

Admitting and owning up to your weaknesses requires a high degree of emotional strength, and it's not a pain-free exercise. But it's the only way to move forward and keep developing and getting better. In a recent *Harvard Business Review* blog article, Bill J. Bonnstetter of Target Training International, Ltd. writes that his company's assessments revealed personal accountability to be one of the five key factors most predictive of an entrepreneurial mindset. (Persuasion, leadership, goal orientation, and interpersonal skills are the others.) He concluded that those who blame other people for failure are most likely to stall in any entrepreneurial effort.

Once you've located the gaps in your talents and skills (emotional or otherwise), you have to find a way to fill them. That's when you have to morph from a skilled self-psychoanalyst into a brilliant talent scout. No matter how smart you are, you need a team of even smarter people around you to grow your business. If you want to build a company that eventually builds itself, you need to figure out how to size people up fairly quickly and admit equally quickly when you've made a mistake.

Developing that scouting ability has proven the saving grace of my career. Time after time, I've hired people without having a specific job in mind for them, just thinking, "Wow, this person is smart and capable. I want her on my team." Almost without exception, these individuals have found their feet quickly and helped me hugely.

It's worth mentioning that I started out with a different tendency: I hired people who were a lot like me. They shared my interests, they saw the world the way I did, and they were good at the same kinds of things I'm good at. I thought it was great to have so many like-minded types on board, until a business coach looked at the situation and told me in no uncertain terms that it was hurting the company. A bunch of people who were just like me couldn't compensate for my weaknesses. The coach's advice: Venture needed a more balanced mix of personalities and competencies, and I should let go about half my staff.

I agonized over how and when to follow through. Having to fire people is one of the worst aspects of running your own business, and in this case it was particularly unpleasant because these weren't terrible employees. The issue was that I'd made a mistake: I shouldn't have hired them in the first place. But as soon as the coach gave me the bad news, I knew instinctively that it was the right call. We just couldn't move forward unless there were people on board who brought something new to the mix. I didn't need more me's. I needed people who would challenge me and tell me when I was wrong.

To digress for a moment, I think a lot of entrepreneurs wind up in this same trap when they're starting out. Part of the problem is that, initially, we feel so grateful to anyone who's willing to come along on the journey. Gratitude blinds us a bit when we're hiring. And then there's the money problem—when you're just getting going, you don't have a whole lot of it. So when someone shows up who seems both reasonably well qualified and willing to accept a salary you can actually afford, well, you leap at the chance to hire him. It's only afterward that you find out he's probably available at your rock-bottom wage because he's not really as qualified as he claimed—or you assumed. But since you can't afford a headhunter, and because you're running around putting out fires all over the place, you tend to forgive more than you should. At least I did, and I doubt I'm the only business owner who's ever made this mistake.

The business coach left me with a tough problem: Which employees needed to go and which should stay? I had an intuitive sense, but my intuition was what had made me hire these people in the first place. I decided I needed to go through an analytical exercise and back up my gut instincts with some metrics. As it turned out, my hunches were almost all correct, but I felt more certain about making the hard calls because I had some actual facts and figures.

My next hires were people who were completely different from me, and they brought a new dimension and energy to our company. We couldn't have grown without them. Interestingly, the more self-aware I've become—the more I'm in touch with my weaknesses and flaws—the less defensive I've been. It's very clear to me now that I'm just not good at certain things, and I need people on my team who are brilliant in those areas. The more honest I am with myself, the stronger my team gets.

* * *

Building on existing strengths and acquiring new skills—ones that have nothing to do with reading a balance sheet and everything to do with reading yourself—may seem like a tall order on top of creating a business. And I won't deny that it is. But independence is not as simple as hanging out a shingle announcing that you're on your own now and ready to accept cash or credit. You need confidence and self-analytic skills. You need resilience and self-reliance. You need self-assurance and humility. Most of all, you need to feel happy steering the train even when you can't see the track ahead—and you need to feel that you can handle the consequences if everything goes off the rails (and it will, at some point or another).

Successful entrepreneurs will tell you that they didn't start out with all these strengths. But if you have the inclination, you can develop them. It's part of throwing yourself into your new endeavour and giving it everything you've got. And if you want to be happy as well as independent, you will.

Chapter 3

The Myth of Work/Life Balance

I was raised as a devout Mormon but left the church when I was in my 30s. Cutting loose from the constraints of my upbringing freed me in all sorts of ways, but losing my religion wasn't as uncomplicated as I initially thought it would be. As a young, entrepreneurial single parent, I discovered that I had quickly traded one Holy Grail for another and, like many of my contemporaries, embraced the cult of work/life balance.

The mythical land of work/life balance looks a little different to everybody, but seems to be governed by one important law: work is work, home life is home life, and never the two shall meet. Cancelling on friends, missing your kid's hockey game because you have an important meeting, or failing to show up for a family gathering are cardinal sins in the work/life balance world. Which means that all-in entrepreneurs are by definition in constant risk of ex-communication.

I can't overstate the pressure many entrepreneurs—women, especially—feel to conform to expectations of work/life balance.

And because entrepreneurship is a lifestyle in which personal and professional dreams are interwoven, when we try to keep work and home life separated, we fail miserably.

First, the Guilt

No matter how hard I tried, I couldn't perform the work life/home life juggling act. I felt overwhelmed and was constantly dropping balls or losing them altogether. I knew what the problem was: me. I just couldn't manage as well as everyone else. So whenever my kids gave me flak for being glued to my BlackBerry on a family vacation, or my friends got angry when I ditched plans with them at the last minute because I had to put out a fire at the office, I felt guilty. Not just a little bit guilty, either. We're talking sickening waves of guilt, which I tried to surf with a whole new raft of resolutions. *I'll be more disciplined and organized. I'll get up an hour earlier so I can fit everything in.* The feeling that I was forever letting people down was really horrible. But the harder I tried to juggle, the more frazzled I became, the more spectacularly I failed, and the more guilty I felt. Eventually, my guilt began to eat me up so much that I realized it was negatively affecting every area of my life.

Looking back, I can't believe how many years I wasted beating myself up about my failure to achieve this elusive work/life balance that glossy magazines assured me was within my grasp, if only I tried hard enough. It took me a long time to realize that all I was really doing was setting myself up for failure. I was never going to make it into that idyllic gated community where entrepreneurs led perfectly balanced lives, for one simple reason: it didn't exist. The idea that I could achieve work/life balance was a myth, right up there with the fantasy that it was possible for me to "have it all." Not only was I destined to fail in my quest to "fit everything in," but trying would make me miserable, or crazy, or quite possibly both.

The Beauty of Imbalance

Rather than trying to meet some externally imposed, impossible-to-meet, one-size-fits-all expectation, I finally realized I'd be far better off if I simply figured out what made me and my kids happiest and my business healthiest—who cared what anyone else thought?—and then did it. My intuition told me balance wouldn't actually make me all that happy. The idea of an existence parcelled into two separate packages of exactly equal size, one labelled "work" and the other labelled "life," started to seem idiotic. I didn't even *want* to live like that, for one simple reason: when I walk through the door of my office, I don't magically turn into another person— I'm the same person at work that I am at home.

For me, and virtually all the contented entrepreneurs I know, work is not a thing apart. It's a part of who we are. For us, our work *is* our life, and we like it that way. Frankly, outside of our families, work is the most fulfilling aspect of our lives. It's also where we feel most in control, which helps explain why we're obsessed with it and find it so hard to tear ourselves away. I don't just mean physically. You don't have to hole up at the office or have a Bluetooth permanently implanted in your ear or dash from one networking event to the next to be at work. When you love what you do, it tends to occupy a lot of mental real estate. Even if you're on a beach in the Caribbean, your brain may be clocking hours at work, reading books on how to improve your leadership style, grinding away on a thorny problem, or brainstorming new possibilities. One of the main differences between the corporate and the entrepreneur-ial lifestyles is that when you work for someone else, you're on the beach wishing you never had to return to work. *Why do I get so little holiday time, for God's sake?* When you're running your own show, you're more likely to be thinking, *Just three more days, then I'm back to the land of decent cell reception.*

In his 40-plus years as an entrepreneur, John Risley says the longest he has ever gone without checking in on his business has been a few hours. And when he is participating in family events, or hanging out with his grandchildren, he's often multi-tasking. "People think I'm distant, but it's not that I don't enjoy my family. It's that, by definition, I'm always thinking about a problem."

And though the demands of an entrepreneurial venture ebb and flow—for instance, the needs of a start-up tend to be more immediate and intense than an established business—entrepre-neurs live a big part of their lives in their heads, especially when they achieve high levels of success.

"You're the catalyst that brings the people and the resources together, and you're the fuel that makes it all work," John says. "People are always looking to you for direction, and so you have a huge responsibility. You can't ever shake that."

Our work is not a cloak we put on and take off. It's woven into the way we think and the way we live our lives. Choosing to be an entrepreneur isn't like choosing a job or an industry or a profession or a career. It is, fundamentally, a lifestyle choice. I see that as the single most important distinction between those who work for themselves and those who don't. When you embrace this way of life, you're not driven by a financial imperative. Obviously you're hoping to make a living, but most entrepreneurs are *not* dreaming they'll make a killing, get rich quick, and retire. Okay, we wouldn't say *no* to making a killing, but what drives us is bigger than that. John Risley calls this entrepreneurial force "a disease": a deeply felt desire to show up every day and create, decide, risk, and grow. Entrepreneurs feel they're embarking on the consummate creative endeavour: they are building a company from scratch and reinventing themselves in the process. The entrepreneurial lifestyle is essentially all about innovation, and as any creative person will tell you, creativity doesn't flourish when you try to box it in. And it doesn't watch the clock.

No one is shocked to learn that a songwriter is forever scribbling down lyrics on scraps of paper, or that a painter is inspired by something he sees on his way to the grocery store. We don't think of them as workaholics. We don't even view those flashes of creativity as work, per se. The round-the-clock call of creativity is just part of the artistic lifestyle. You don't schedule visits from the muse. Nor do you tell the muse, *Sorry, this is date night, I can't take your call.*

Entrepreneurial creativity works much the same way, which is to say, all the time. What we're creating is value and capital and products and services, not poetry and painting and music and drama. So we don't have the licence to say that our work is our life. When an artist says that, it sounds romantic. When an entrepreneur says it, it's viewed as a cop-out, just another excuse for taking a work call during a romantic dinner.

But the important thing is not how others view your work. It's how *you* define and understand what you're doing. And once you give yourself permission to see it for what it is—a creative expression of your personality, essentially—it's pretty obvious that it makes no sense at all to pretend that you can achieve work/life balance. That would require prying apart two aspects of your existence that are completely intertwined.

Coming to this understanding was a process that took me years. When I decided that this was something to celebrate, rather than be ashamed of and try desperately to compensate for, I began to enjoy the experience of independence wholeheartedly. Before, it had been a guilty pleasure, almost, loving my work as I did. Certainly I felt I should be apologizing for it. But I came to see that, rather than hive off my passion for my work and feel I should keep it separate, I'd be far better off—as would everyone around me—if I found ways to *incorporate* my family, friends, interests, and personal values into my business life. If I wanted to feel happy and fulfilled as an entrepreneur *and* as a human being, I had to write off the ideal of work/life balance as N/A. Just not applicable to me.

That has been very freeing, like shrugging off a straitjacket. Years ago I felt guilty every time I had to cancel a coffee date with a friend—something that happened almost weekly. Today, I forbid myself to feel guilty over cancelling meet-ups. I also book far fewer. I've learned that saying "no" from the outset is way easier than saying "sorry, but I have to cancel. Again."

Once you accept that it's amazing that your work *is* your life, and begin to think about all the ways to *include* your various duties, interests, and passions in your entrepreneurial ventures instead of searching for ways to *exclude* work from other aspects of your life, it's hugely liberating. You'll also be surprised by how much more productive you are when you're no longer wasting time trying to erect the equivalent of the Berlin Wall between what's personal and what's professional.

When I began to think about orchestrating a lifestyle rhythm that worked for me, what came to mind was the unpredictability and random beauty of jazz. A jazz riff is all about leaving the comfort of a familiar harmonic structure to set off on a freer musical adventure. It's about pushing the envelope knowing that there's just enough structure to prevent you from lapsing into chaos. As wild and discordant as it may be at times, you'll be okay if you accept certain basic principles—and practise religiously.

Getting Comfortable with Discomfort

Christine Magee, the president and co-founder of Sleep Country Canada, puts it another way. When someone asked her in an online Q&A how she struck a balance between the demands of work and family life without experiencing burnout or marital stress, she said she'd come to believe that balance is simply "getting comfortable with the idea that I am always going to be a little uncomfortable." I think that's exactly right.

The late Nora Ephron, another consummate entrepreneur, arrived at a similar conclusion. Besides being a wife, mother, beloved friend, and mentor to many, Ephron was a journalist, essayist, playwright, screenwriter, novelist, producer, director, and blogger at different times in her career. When she delivered an address to the students at Wellesley College, she told the young female graduates that they really could "have it all"—but only if they accepted that their lives would be a little messy and learned to "embrace the mess." She went on to advise them to "rejoice in the complications. It will not be anything like what you think it will be like, but surprises are good for you. And don't be frightened: you can always change your mind. I know: I've had four careers and three husbands."

Maybe you're thinking entrepreneurs have some magic formula for embracing mess, but I assure you we don't. Most of the time, we just muddle through. When I started out, I was a single parent with four young kids. I'm a neat freak, so I always had a neat house, but my life was still chaotic. But I wasn't embracing it. I wasn't embracing *anything* except the notion of survival. In those days, guilt was my only long-time companion. When I was working, I felt guilty about shortchanging my kids. When I was with my kids, I felt guilty about neglecting my business. It was a total no-win. It's only as I've grown older that I've figured out how to be a better parent *and* entrepreneur simultaneously.

One important lesson I have learned is to be *present* wherever I am. When I spend time with my kids, I now try either to turn off my cell phone or to look at it far less frequently so I can actually be with them and not constantly checking emails or taking calls. I try not to drone on about the office too much, either. I also came to realize over time that sometimes being a mother is just about being reliably, consistently reachable—even when you're travelling, even when the deal is closing, even when you're beyond exhausted.

Consistency and reachability will be easier if you ditch conventional definitions of good parental behaviour. For instance, modern parenting etiquette suggests that checking email and taking phone calls during your kid's soccer game is emotionally damaging for them and you. Julie Cole sees it differently. Julie cofounded Mabel's Labels, a manufacturer of custom labels for children's clothing, after her oldest son, who is now 13, was diagnosed with autism at age three. Julie was trained as a lawyer, but figured owning her business would give her more flexibility when it came to attending doctor's appointments or advocating for her son at school. Although she had three other business partners to share the workload, Julie says she quickly learned that "having flexibility didn't equal having more time." To complicate time management matters further, Julie went on to have five more children while she was building her business, whose products are now distributed via Wal-Mart Canada and Target USA.

Eschewing conventional parenting rules and communicating with her kids about the realities of the entrepreneurial life has allowed her to devote herself full-time to both her family and her business. Exhibit A: her ever-present, always-on smartphone. "My kids know that if I didn't have my gadget, I wouldn't be able to watch their hockey games." Before any game or practice, she'll take her kids aside and explain that if they look up and happen to see her talking on her phone or sending an email, it's because the matter is urgent. And the best part? "They totally get it. They're happy I'm there." Julie finds other ways to streamline operations on the home front that might also ruffle the feathers of people intent on playing by the social rules. Five of her kids play hockey. Rather than driving to five different practices a night, she put one of her daughters on a boys' team and moved another one of her daughters up a division so she could play on a team with her sister. Her house is "clean but messy," and she rarely hosts a dinner that isn't a potluck. "You've got to do what makes sense for you— not what works for other people."

I'd be lying if I pretended I don't still have days when I feel overwhelmed. I do and probably always will. But whatever anxiety I feel is lightened by the fact that independence comes fully loaded with many fantastic perks, one of which is that no two of my days are the same. Some people would hate the lack of predictability and yearn for more structure, the comfort of routine. For me, though, the lack of sameness makes me feel wholly alive. I feel so much more excited about life and fully engaged at 56 than I did at 26. Feeling stretched beyond my capacity on some days is the price I have to pay for that privilege, and I'm more than willing to pay it.

When people ask when I'm going to slow down and retire, I find the question confounding. Why would I want to, ever? I think I'll be trying to make deals and fundraise for my favourite charities on my deathbed. I'll be doing that not because I don't know the true meaning of life, but because, actually, I do know the true meaning of *my* life. What propels me forward is the desire to spend my time doing what I love, making a difference where I can, and living full-tilt. When work and life are indistinguishable, retirement equals death.

Anyone who considers their work their calling views retirement in much the same way. In 2012, when, at 82, Christopher Plummer became the oldest star ever to win an Oscar, he told reporters after his win that working recharged him and he planned to continue for at least another decade: "I'm going to drop dead wherever I am, on stage or on the set. We don't retire in our profession, thank God."

Most creative types don't. And I include myself, and all entrepreneurs, in that category.

It's Your Hourglass—Handle with Care

The sad truth is that far too many people spend their days in jobs they just don't like very much. In a recent survey of more than 400 workers in Canada and the United States conducted by Right Management, a subsidiary of the giant staffing firm ManpowerGroup, nearly two-thirds of respondents said they were unhappy at work. Only 19 percent reported feeling content.

These are astonishing numbers when you stop to think about it: for eight hours a day—minimum, given how the working day has expanded—the majority of the working population is unhappy. When you're stuck in a job you don't love, satisfaction is all about the externals: the regular paycheque, the benefits, having a badge of identity and belonging, and job security (an increasingly meaningless concept in this economy). You give up on the possibility of finding enrichment or of feeling truly energized at work, because you know it's never going to happen. Now, some people are okay with that. They never wanted more.

But for others, that sense of disconnection between who they are as individuals and what they do for a living is unbearably unpleasant. It wears you down, like little drops of water on stone, to spend hour after hour doing something that doesn't provide the level of emotional or spiritual return you're looking for. Work becomes a drag, something to be survived.

Years before Michael Merrithew bought a small travel agency and grew it into Merit Travel, the largest specialty travel company in the country, he was one of those workers doing time in jobs he didn't really like. It's not that the jobs were dead-end. Far from it. He worked first in the training and marketing departments in the aviation, telecom, and marketing industries, and then moved on to a business development job in advertising. But what started out as a sense of restlessness morphed into extreme discomfort for Michael, who was trying to ply his entrepreneurial instincts in a corporate setting.

"I was constantly making recommendations, but really wasn't in the position to be able to act on them. I started to wonder whether I was having any impact whatsoever."

One afternoon, while sitting outside a client's office waiting for an appointment, he saw an ad in *The Globe and Mail* for a travel agency that was for sale. It said, "Be Your Own Boss." He followed up on the ad, bought the travel agency, and has never again questioned whether his daily efforts are having an impact. As an entrepreneur, he knows that he calls the shots and bears the consequences of those decisions.

Of course, all entrepreneurs have problems and challenges, and there are parts of our job we don't exactly relish, like having to fire people. But entrepreneurs don't have that whipped-dog look you see on the faces of people who hate their jobs. For the most part, we find our work extraordinarily fulfilling. In fact, a sense of anticipation jet-propels most entrepreneurs out of bed most days. We want to get to work because it's engaging, challenging, and fun. For me, work is the place where I feel most fully myself, and I think that's true for most entrepreneurs.

That's why you don't hear us grousing about work/life balance, at least not in the same way that unhappily employed people do. In fact, I think most entrepreneurs don't really want "balance." It's freedom we're after. We wish there were more hours in the day, yes, but not because we're desperate to relax. We'd just like time to accomplish even more. We're not fans of limits, period. And time is limiting. It's also a commodity we can't create more of.

"I know some people who have lots of time and others who have lots of money, but few who have both," says Charles Chang. "I wanted to create a lifestyle that could give me time and the money to be able to really enjoy that time." When he launched his business in 2001, Charles decided he would set up his business in such a way that he would be able to take one extra week of vacation each year, and that he would avoid working on Wednesdays in order to spend time with his wife and three children. By carefully setting up processes and systems, hiring smart vice-presidents and putting them in charge of profit and losses within their own departments, and training his senior staff to function without his constant oversight and supervision, Charles is able to take 14 weeks of holiday a year, and he rarely works on Wednesdays.

"I have so many passions," Charles says. "Business is one of them, but I'm also passionate about fishing, cycling, travelling, and spending time with my family. The magic of being an entrepreneur is that you have the ability to control time so you can fit in the things that are important to you."

As a species, entrepreneurs are hyper-aware of time. I also live with a sense of urgency, as though time is running out to cram in all the living I want to do, and that feeling has only increased with age. Many people believe that successful entrepreneurs live by the maxim that time is money, and to some extent that's true. Making money is not irrelevant—we're running businesses, after all. But most entrepreneurs I know, myself included, aren't driven by a desire to go rake in more cash. We're driven by a desire to get the most of life that we can, and I think because we are both dreamers *and* doers, we have bigger ideas about what's possible. I don't have one eye on the clock because I want to make more money. In fact, I think it would be sad to feel that I had to link every time-management decision I make to its potential financial return. When I consider how to apportion my time, I try to figure out whether what I'm thinking of doing will *enrich* my life, not whether it will make me richer. I believe most successful entrepreneurs think the same way.

When Work Is an Addiction

As much as I love my work, I also know how easily the line between work and workaholism can become blurred for an entrepreneur. There's a risk that what starts as a passion can become a full-blown addiction. Then your work isn't intertwined with your life. It eclipses everything else.

On *Dragons' Den*, I've seen that scenario play out again and again. People come on the show obsessed with their business to the point where their personal lives are in total freefall. Sometimes it's evident that a couple's relationship is a casualty of one or both partners' entrepreneurial ambitions. I remember one couple who had become so fixated on their business that they had nothing left. I could see the terrible financial and emotional toll their obsession had taken on their marriage, and I said, "This has been really hard on you, hasn't it?" They both broke down instantly. It was just heartbreaking. In their case, despite all they'd been through, they still loved each other and still had a shot at happiness together. But sometimes you see a guy come on the show who has fallen so blindly in love with his business idea that when he finally lifts his head and looks around, his wife and kids are long gone.

Even as I warn, Cassandra-like, about the dangers of becoming a work junkie, I can see my kids rolling their eyes. They want me to tell the truth: there have been many times in my life when I have been so addicted to work, I probably would have benefited from an intervention. I remember days when my kids would come directly to the Venture office after school and ride the halls on the mail cart while I worked on presentations. Needless to say, we ate more pizza than was probably healthy.

Even Charles Chang, who takes summers off (though he does check in once a week), has battled his own workaholic demons. When he started his business he focused on it almost exclusively—even when he was taking care of his kids during his Wednesdays off. He wore himself down so much that he got shingles, lived with chronic cold sores, and gained loads of weight. Learning to shut off business—even in the beginning at least, if only for an afternoon—changed his life. "It took years of training, but doing it is so important. Otherwise you drive yourself and everyone around you crazy," he says.

Cliff Oxford, who runs the Oxford Center for Entrepreneurs, wrote candidly on this subject in the *New York Times.* When you're growing a company, he said, you're thinking about work in the shower, on vacation, at the dinner table. Once you experience some success, you may "become an addict, but instead of getting drunk at a bar, you get high on work. And that is fine until you have to go home and deal with routine family matters like changing diapers, taking out the trash, or attending meetings of the PTA or, God forbid, the homeowner's association. You are always in a hurry, and everybody else is so slow."

One evening, his human resources director called him into her office saying they needed to talk. He knew that hearing those words from an HR director—even if you're the chief executive—is never a good thing. And it wasn't. She was giving him an official warning: he was married to his work, and he needed to think long and hard about whether he wanted to sacrifice the rest of his life for the business. Oxford dismissed the conversation as alarmist, because he was having a great time and figured he had everything under control. Five years later, he had a bunch of plaques on his wall testifying to his astronomical success, and one divorce decree. "This is the danger of the balance propaganda," Oxford wrote. "You think you can have it all, and you wind up losing what means most to you."

It's an all-too-familiar theme. Oxford works with hundreds of fast-growth entrepreneurs and, after seeing this tragedy replayed again and again, he decided to try to intervene and help others who appeared to be in danger of losing their families. However, he was about as successful as his HR director was with him. Only 2 or 3 percent of the entrepreneurs actually made any lifestyle adjustments—about the same success rate, he discovered, as heroin users have in rehab. How does he know that? Well, he invited a medical doctor with an MBA to speak at a conference he'd organized for a group of entrepreneurs. To illustrate how the brain reacts to pleasure, she showed brain scans of heroin addicts, people with attention-deficit disorder, people engaged in intimate acts—and entrepreneurs. She demonstrated that the same brain stimulants that send heroin addicts "back to the needle" are the ones that fuel entrepreneurs' drive and capacity for work fulfillment.

If work is a rush, and it exerts such a powerful pull over you that you wind up alienating everyone around you, what's the cure? Like anything in life, it comes down to making deliberate choices, which is why I'm always interested in the ones that other entrepreneurs have made, and the lessons they've learned along the way. Diane English, who was profiled in "Makers: Women Who Make America," a fascinating PBS documentary and online initiative about women who changed their country, was one of the first female executive producers in prime-time television. She's best known for creating *Murphy Brown*, the hit television series starring Candice Bergen that ran on CBS from 1988 to 1998. English, too, believes the notion of balance is overrated. She argues that there are simply going to be times in your life when you can't achieve balance and shouldn't even try: "If you've got a dream and a goal, sometimes you've just got to go for it, because if you make compromises, you're not necessarily going to get there. And then there are other times in your life when you can step back . . . I've never been very good at trying to make all those things happen at one time. I don't think anybody's any good at it."

Rather than viewing her life as a teeter-totter that she's forever trying—and failing—to balance just so, she prefers to view it as a book, and her life stages as its chapters. Flipping through it, she explains, she sees a long series of chapters that were all about her dream of creating a hit television show. Interspersed, there are chapters about recharging and reconnecting with friends and family.

Like Diane English, many entrepreneurs say that balance is the enemy of excellence. Perhaps that's why a lot of famously successful entrepreneurs didn't marry or start families until they'd already achieved a certain degree of success. Bill Gates didn't get married until he was about to step down as CEO of Microsoft. Steve Jobs had already achieved rock-star status when he tied the knot. And Spanx founder Sara Blakely also chose not to dilute her focus while she was still building her company. She didn't meet her entrepreneur husband Jesse Itzler until 2006, when their businesses were both well established. (His resumé includes a stint as a rapper; Itzler is the creator of the NBA slogan "I love this game," and the co-founder of Marquis Jet, which leases private planes.) What if they'd met five years earlier? He once told journalist Richard Bradley in an article for Worth.com that either their businesses would have survived or their relationship would have—but not both. Still, their lives were busy when they first met, and they lived in two different cities. How did they make it work? They each had great management in place, according to Itzler, so they "basically put everything on hold, business-wise, for six months." They went all in, focusing on their relationship. According to Blakely, they were both old enough to know that how they felt about each other was "really rare." They didn't want to waste what they had by "not prioritizing. We just did whatever we needed to do to be together."

Of course, it's easier to make these kinds of conscious choices when you're already successful. You can throw money at the problem, and you have the option of delegating. But you don't have to be world famous to junk the idea of balance and, as Diane English did, think of your life in terms of chapters, instead. Some chapters will focus on business; some will focus on family; some will focus on your love life. The order they come in is entirely up to you.

* * *

These days, everyone is strapped for time. We're all finding it a challenge, regardless of whether we're entrepreneurs or not. A recent Canadian Index of Wellbeing report confirms what most of us already know intuitively: Canadians are increasingly struggling to meet the competing demands of a smartphone-enabled 24/7 workplace, and increasingly sacrificing our relaxation and leisure time in order to attend to the more pressing demands of children and aging parents who need support. Women, especially, are feeling the time crunch.

So figuring it all out isn't easy. But it is doable, even for an entrepreneur. And once you do crack the code, by which I mean the one that works for *you*, it will be so worth it. Just don't try to do the impossible, like pretend to yourself that it's possible to "fit everything in" simultaneously. That's one guilt trip you don't need to take.

If you allow yourself to believe that you're entitled to do work that you love—work created by your talents, tied to your unique identity and values, and fuelled by your passion—you no longer have to live in a world where you are constantly chasing after fake ideals like work/life balance. You get to put that demoralizing, pointless, and ultimately crazy-making nonsense behind you. You get to have a love affair, instead: with your work *and* your life as a whole. If you're careful to listen to your instincts and question conventional wisdom, set priorities, and make thoughtful choices, eventually you'll figure out how to design a lifestyle that suits you.

So what if it doesn't look like everybody else's? So what if others judge you for it? Who cares? You're independent now, and so is the way you think.

Chapter 4

Slow Down, Think It Through

Most entrepreneurs I know are impatient. We may spend months or years percolating a potential business idea, but once we've made that internal commitment to launch, we need to start—yesterday. In the game of life, entrepreneurs are sprinters. We often work with explosive energy, we're driven to move our ideas forward quickly, and we hate anything that slows us down. But our inherent need for speed can be our undoing because overnight success is rare. My businesses took decades to build (and I still have lots of work to do). And I've met enough entrepreneurs to know that for every rapid riser like Facebook's Mark Zuckerberg or Google's Sergey Brin, there are 10 of me. Which means that, while entrepreneurs may have the instincts of sprinters, we need to train ourselves for a marathon.

Let's say you know you have what it takes to be an entrepreneur. You were born with the right temperament. You have the right emotional skills. You understand that work/life balance is a crock. That doesn't necessarily mean it's time to quit your job or start another venture. All it really means is that the idea of living creatively and independently makes you think, *hell yeah.* But that's just the tip of the iceberg. Don't get me wrong—as an entrepreneur, you've got to pay attention to your instincts. But you'll most likely get into trouble if you make the big leap with nothing more than your gut to guide you.

What you have to do next is put your sprinter instincts on hold for a while and *think it through.* It's not sexy, and most entrepreneurs I know (present company included) are too impatient to do this naturally. But talk to anyone who's been in this game long enough. They'll tell you that learning how to patiently think through your decisions is critical. Because there *are* costs, ones that can be ruinous if you're not expecting them.

I know you may not want to hear this. Many of the would-be entrepreneurs I meet have stars in their eyes about the lifestyle and simply aren't interested in hearing about the downside. I totally get the desire to romanticize independence. There *is* something inherently romantic about the idea of living your life on your own terms, especially if you feel you're stuck in a rut and are generally dissatisfied with your life. But as much as I appreciate the rewards of the entrepreneurial lifestyle, the truth is that the day-to-day reality of running your own show is not at all romantic.

The goal here isn't to rain on your parade. Optimism is a must for entrepreneurs, and you're going to need endless reserves of it if you decide to go ahead or are currently in the thick of it. But there's informed optimism, and then there's uninformed optimism. One helps you move forward when the going gets tough; the other leaves you reeling from one unexpected setback to the next, wondering why on earth all this negative stuff keeps happening to such a positive person.

It's better to know what to expect. And it's better to ask your-self the tough questions now, to see if this really is the kind of life you want.

Are You Willing to Ride a Roller Coaster, Blindfolded?

Are you contemplating life as an entrepreneur? You know it won't be easy. But until you actually get started, you have no idea how hard it's going to be. You know it takes money, time, and personal sacrifices. But it will take more money, time, and personal sacrifices than you can possibly imagine. You may think you're prepared, but trust me (and also every entrepreneur I interviewed for this book): you're not. No one ever is. And the funny thing is, whether you're starting your first business, or your fifth, there will always be hidden roadblocks positioned in a way that could derail you.

That's because there will be twists and turns you can't possibly anticipate. Some will be strictly related to supply and demand and broader economic and regulatory changes that affect your particular business for better or for worse. But others will be related to your own capacity to respond to psychological and emotional challenges. How will you manage the stress and anxiety of a launch? What if your partner, or a crucial investor, suddenly wants out? Or your spouse says, "It's me or the business"? You will be tested in many ways. And many times, you will have no one else to rely on. And no one else to blame.

Independence is a roller coaster you ride alone—blindfolded, with no certainty about what's going to happen next, even though you built the damn thing. When I first boarded, I had no clue how much courage and humility and sheer bloody-minded determination it would take simply to hang on. If I had known, I'm not sure I would have chosen to proceed. But I'm so glad I did, because it's turned out to be an amazing ride: occasionally nauseating and scary, but also exhilarating and challenging in ways that make me feel fully alive. And now that I'm accustomed to the ups and downs, I can't imagine doing anything else.

But you might not feel that way—particularly if you start a business against all odds, give it your all, and don't get the success you envisioned. If you're interested in the destination rather than the journey, you might not enjoy lurching between peaks and valleys. You might like the idea of that, but in reality you could find yourself yearning for a little more certainty and predictability, and a less bumpy ride.

So are you ready for that ride? Is your gut giving you the big thumbs up? Great. Now you need to step back, simmer down, and carefully think it through. And if you're already on the journey, you need to take some time to remember that this ride can be one that has higher highs and lower lows than you ever expected.

Do You Hate Your Job? Or Do You Want to Build a New Life?

I think there are good reasons to become an entrepreneur, and then there are some not-so-good reasons. One I'd include in the latter category is hating your job. I empathize deeply with anyone who feels stuck in a lousy job or has to report to a boss who's a jerk or petty tyrant. But having said that, I think it's a really, really bad idea to try to start a business when your primary goal is to escape the hell you're in now.

Job dissatisfaction may be one factor in your decision, but if it's the only one, think again. As we'll see later on, some entrepreneurs leave great, well-paying jobs behind when they strike out on their own. But the reason they do that is not because they're compelled by a desire to *escape* their situation. Rather, they're driven by a desire to *create* a new one. And once consumed with that desire to build something new, resistance is futile.

Charles Chang is a great example. After graduating from university with a business degree, he landed a marketing job in Vancouver for a company that manufactures cardboard boxes. Charles was "ecstatic" to have a job in his field of study and quickly climbed the corporate ladder. Within a few years, he was being mentored by the firm's president and making more than $200,000 a year: not bad for the kid who once pulled in five bucks a sunfish. But as much as he loved the money, the best part of the job was what he learned. Because of his close relationship with his boss, he got a front-row seat on the operational side of the business and learned things like how to prepare cash-flow projections and what to look for in a quality control system. "I really benefited from that experience because I wasn't a measurement and metrics kind of a guy. I was more of a touchy-feely creative type. He taught me that side of the business." But as the years wore on, Charles's headstrong, entrepreneurial streak kicked in more and more. "I started noticing that when I had ideas people didn't agree with, I would pout and not be good to work with." He knew in his gut it was time to fly the coop.

When Charles handed in his resignation, his boss—who had been expecting his protege to strike out on his own—gave Charles an offer he couldn't refuse: choose his own hours and tele-work part-time for a year while he launched Vega, his supplements company. The offer helped him get through a very lean start-up year, and he still meets his old mentor for lunch once a quarter to talk shop.

Intrapreneurs—entrepreneurial types who are working in a corporate setting or for another entrepreneur—have a lot to learn from Charles's experience. The corporate world—with all its processes and systems—can be a great training ground for aspiring entrepreneurs. Learn what you can and build good relationships with your colleagues and mentors. They will come in handy if you do decide to go your own way. Which means that even if you are working in a job you know you want to quit, it's paramount to maintain good working relationships and not burn your bridges. In my experience, people can smell disengagement a mile away. And that's why Charles's story makes such a great point.

Why did he quit the company he worked for? Not because he hated his job. He left because he had a deep need to be in a situation where he could call the shots and follow through on his ideas. You need to have that fire in your belly to enjoy being an entrepreneur. If the main thing burning you up is hatred of your current job/boss/co-workers, it couldn't possibly sustain you through the tough times you'd face on your own.

Are You Tempted to Hedge Your Bets?

Recently, I had a conversation with some business partners about whether there's a litmus test for entrepreneurship, a surefire way to know whether someone is cut out for it. Someone said that an unusually large appetite for risk is the essential ingredient. Someone else argued that the willingness to make your business more important than everything else in life, including your family, is the only sure sign. My position was that I always know somebody's not cut out for the lifestyle and never will be if he tells me he has a full-time job and is trying to launch his new business as a hobby. There's no such thing as a part-time entrepreneur, in my opinion. You're all in, or you might as well go home.

This discussion sparked a heated debate: What about a woman who's her family's sole means of support? Was I calling her a faux entrepreneur simply because she didn't have the option of risking everything, financially? What about the Charles Changs of the world, who maintain a part-time job while they launch their businesses? Are they faux entrepreneurs? Well, no. We all have to do what we have to do to survive and put food on the table. But it's also true that there is no ideal time to leave the safety net, and it's the willingness to take the safety net–free leap that is the sign of a true entrepreneur.

My point isn't to sneer at people who value security. My guess is that people who do are, on average, probably more sane and balanced than entrepreneurs are. And I know for sure that they can do meaningful work where they move the ball forward for themselves, for their companies, and, depending on the type of work they're doing, for the rest of us, too.

My point is simply to encourage you to be fiercely honest with yourself about your level of commitment. You have to understand that choosing independence means you're going to be required to burn some bridges and, thereafter, walk a high wire—with no safety net. This is true whether you are leaving a marriage, moving to a new town, or giving up secure employment to strike out on your own. If you find yourself trying to think of ways to hedge your bets or hang on to the security that you have now, don't ignore your instincts. They're telling you that you're just not ready.

Can You Relax Your Standards in Other Areas of Your Life?

Ask yourself: "Am I really able, at this point in my life, to make a huge emotional investment?" Let's say, for instance, that you're having trouble juggling home and work, and you decide that life might be a whole lot easier if you had more control over your work schedule. *Maybe*, you're thinking, *I can care for my kids and create a business that's tailored to fit my needs, not some corporation's needs?*

On the surface, this arrangement seems like the perfect solution to the conundrum of work/life balance. It did for Julie Cole, who founded Mabel's Labels in part because she wanted to have the flexibility to handle appointments with her autistic son. But remember Julie's lesson: flexibility doesn't get your work done for you. In order to devote yourself fully to being a great parent and a great entrepreneur, simultaneously, you have to make a huge and equal emotional and logistical commitment to *both* roles. Trying to do that will probably kill you (unless your kids are at boarding school; the kind where parents are strictly forbidden to visit).

The solution is not to choose one role over the other. I'd be a hypocrite to tell you that, because it's not what I did. I know it's possible, though not easy, to be a good enough mother and a good enough entrepreneur at the same time. But there's only one way to do it: start from the premise that you don't have endless reserves of emotional capital, and acknowledge that launching a new business is highly emotionally draining. Then relax your expectations of your performance in both roles—pretty drastically, if you're anything like me—and pledge to forgive yourself readily when, nevertheless, you still fall short. You have to get good with the idea of being good enough, rather than perfect or excellent or irreproachable. Before I got involved in business, I used to call myself "Molly Mormon" because of the effort and energy I devoted to homemaking—fresh bread, handmade pies. Even though they were made out of necessity—because we could afford little else but what we made from scratch—I prided myself on preparing delicious homemade foods for my family. But when I was building Venture, my cooking went out the window. Often the only time I could make meals like I once did was on long weekends. The "old me" would have been mortified. But I had to let that part of me go in order to step into my new identity as an up-and-coming entrepreneur. Now cooking is something I look forward to when I have down time and can relax and enjoy the experience. I still love it. I just can't do it every day.

If you can't find it in yourself to let go of something, you'll fall into the trap of thinking, *Of course, I have to go on every field trip my child's school arranges; that's the whole reason I became an entrepreneur. I'll make up for it by working until 3 a.m.* Or thinking, *I've got to exceed clients' demands—otherwise they'll think I'm unprofessional. Seven more hours in front of the TV probably won't hurt the kids in the long run.* Either way, you'll wind up feeling far more guilty than you would in a corporate job, where at least there'd be someone else to blame (and a few paid days off every year).

Can You Handle Criticism?

About 18 months after having a baby and three years after launching Belvedere Place Development, a road-building business, Kelsey Ramsden won a multi-million-dollar contract to repair a section of the Alaska Highway in northern British Columbia—Fort Saint John, to be exact. The job promised to be especially daunting because she would be completing it without her usual team of experienced workers: her regular employees were working in other parts of the province, so she'd hired a group of heavy-equipment operators she'd never worked with. To make matters worse, a local mine had hired away the city's most experienced workers. Which left Kelsey facing the biggest project of her career with a rookie team. Between her crew and northern BC's short summer, Kelsey would be working 16- and 18-hour days to get the job done—and to have any hope of securing more contracts from her client. Meanwhile, her husband had just announced that he wanted to start a business in his hometown of London, Ontario. The couple faced a tough choice—move the family to Fort Saint John, where she would be working around the clock and her husband would have to be a stay-at-home dad; or split the family up: she'd stay in Fort Saint John and finish the contract; he'd move to London with daughter Sophie, where he could open his business and tap his family and friends for help with the baby.

For Kelsey, there was only one option. In order to bid on the job, she had had to secure a multi-million-dollar bond, and she'd put up the family's home and all their assets as security. If the job went south, her family would be penniless. "I was committed. There was no way I could pull out or let it fail." So at the beginning of the construction season, Kelsey kissed her husband and 18-month-old daughter goodbye, got on a plane, and flew to northern BC. She worked around the clock for the next six months. Because she was the most senior person on the job, she was able to get home for only two days to visit her husband and daughter—about three months into the contract. She spent many nights crying in her bathroom, exhausted from work, proud of how the project was going, but homesick beyond belief. "It was really hard. I missed them like crazy. But I knew it was what I signed up for," Kelsey confesses.

Other people didn't see it that way. Kelsey says her friends and even some family members criticized her for her decision to leave her daughter. And when she went back to work two days after having her second child, a close friend asked why she kept having babies if she didn't want to look after them. In the beginning, Kelsey says, she felt "pure rage" when people criticized her for "putting her business first." But over time, she's learned to stop explaining her decisions to—or internalizing criticism from—people who don't understand what it means for her to be all in.

"They couldn't see the vision that I have in my head for the life I want for me and my family. Nothing I say can make them see that. So I just gave up trying to explain myself."

Do You Have Faith in Yourself?

It's one thing to have a vision. It's another to have a vision that is so bright and consuming that you have no choice other than to follow it. Having an unwavering belief in your vision gives you the conviction that even if everything falls apart, you will survive. For an entrepreneur, this messianic self-belief is a critical ingredient. It's the fire under your butt that drives you forward.

Let me tell you a story about Dave Buckle. I first met Dave on *Dragons' Den* when he and his business partner, Trevor Fronchak, came on the show to pitch Funk-Off, a natural deodorant designed for people who have body piercings. (It seems body piercings create dead cells that can emit a foul odour—who says that commercial television can't be educational?) Dave has a tattoo on his forearm that says "Believe," and as soon as you meet him, you understand it's not just for show. The guy believes in himself and his project with a faith that borders on the religious.

One Saturday morning in 2012, Dave was heading to the grocery store in his hometown of Port Stanley, Ontario. Both his kids were in the van, and he was flipping through radio stations when he heard an announcement that *Dragons' Den* producers were in town that day, conducting auditions to find would-be entrepreneurs to pitch on the next season's show. They were holding an open casting call at Windermere Manor in London—the exact intersection where Dave was waiting for the light to change when he heard the announcement.

Now, Dave had been not just a fan but really a student of the show for seven years. He had always imagined that *Dragons' Den* would be in his future, so he figured this was a sign from the universe. Even though he was wearing blue jeans and work boots, and all he and Trevor had at that stage was a newly hatched product and a crude packaging prototype they'd cobbled together with a bit of body jewellery, a computer printout, and some paste, Dave decided to go for it.

He dropped off his kids with his wife, Sarah, who was at one of their stores in a mall in London; the couple owns a business that sells body jewellery. Shortly afterward, he was back at Windermere Manor filling out forms and taking a number, as if he'd just landed on the set of *American Idol*. Three weeks after that, on his way back from a trip to Thailand to sort out some manufacturing issues, his plane touched down at Pearson Airport in Toronto and his cell phone rang: it was an invitation to appear on the show.

To me, this is a quintessential entrepreneurial story. Dave wasn't really "ready" to do a pitch. All he had was a nascent product and a willingness to put himself out there. But instead of talking himself out of auditioning, which would have been so easy to do, he took a shot.

There's another word for the unshakeable self-belief that Dave showed: charisma. Don't underestimate its power, especially when you're just starting out. When I began to pitch investors, there really wasn't any good reason why the banks and individuals I approached should have loaned me money. In fact, there were quite a few good reasons they shouldn't have. I didn't have a track record as an entrepreneur. I didn't show up with a fancy PowerPoint presentation. And I'm sure I didn't present my ideas in the most articulate fashion. And yet I did secure loans.

I think that aside from detecting the nugget of a good idea in my pitch, they valued the fact that I wore my passion on my sleeve. Some people view sincerity as a lack of sophistication and think that enthusiasm is corny. Others view those same qualities as hallmarks of authenticity, and those are the types of people who didn't dismiss me as small-time. Because I believed so much in what I was trying to create, they believed in me, too.

Now that I'm on the other side of the equation and in a position to invest in start-ups, I see what a powerful force charisma can be. It comes in many forms, ranging from intensely cerebral to down-to-earth charm, but the common denominator is always the sort of self-belief that lights up a room and commands attention. Though I'm pretty hard-headed about the projects I choose to invest in—this is business, after all, not charity—on more than one occasion on our show, a contestant's charisma has tipped the balance for me.

I remember very clearly when Larry Finnson and Chris Emery came on *Dragons' Den* to pitch OMG Candy. They'd already built a successful company in the same category, but didn't yet have any sales and were asking for a lot of money: a quarter of a million dollars. On paper, it looked like a pretty dumb investment (particularly for someone trying to maintain her weight but who'd feel ethically bound to sample the product on a regular if not daily basis). But in person, the two men were so passionate about what they were building and so visibly excited by the possibilities of their new venture that I decided they were the real deal. I went with my gut and decided to invest. It turned out to be a great deal for me as well as for them, and yet another reminder of how important it is, as an entrepreneur, to have faith in yourself.

How Do You Feel About Regrets?

Let's say you're intellectually ready to make the commitment to entrepreneurialism. You've done your homework, crunched the numbers, cobbled together the financing, checked off all the boxes, and reached the point where you simply can't find a good argument against trying to see if your business will fly. You believe with every fibre of your being that you have a killer idea nobody's thought of before—one that the world needs. And yet . . . every time you peer over the edge of the cliff, your stomach does wheelies and you pull back.

It feels as if you'll be stuck in limbo forever and will never find the clarity or courage to act. You start to wonder if at some point there'll be a moment when the clouds suddenly clear and you just *know*. And if there is such a moment, how can you speed up the process a little bit and make it happen faster?

It may cheer you to know that Jeff Bezos found himself in exactly the same quandary when he considered leaving his lucrative Wall Street job to start Amazon.com. In an interview posted on YouTube, he tells the story of how once he had come up with his business plan, he told his boss that he was going to do something crazy: start an online bookstore. His boss suggested they go for a walk to talk things over. After a two-hour stroll through Central Park, he told Bezos that the idea sounded great but, in fact, sounded even better for somebody who didn't already have a really good job. Bezos's boss convinced him to think things over for 48 hours before deciding.

Jeff Bezos already had his wife's unequivocal support, which he appreciated greatly because when she married him, she thought she was signing on for a life with a fairly stable guy with a reassuringly predictable career trajectory. He knew that if he chucked his job to throw himself into a start-up, he'd be gambling not just with his future but with hers, too. So he needed to be absolutely sure it was the right thing to do.

Which is why he came up with a system to help him make this momentous life decision: the Regret Minimization Framework. Bezos's idea was that he wanted to minimize the number of regrets he'd have at the end of his life. So to try to figure out whether to start an online company, he imagined himself at the age of 80: How would he feel about it then? He knew instantly that he wouldn't regret having tried, even if he failed. But he would regret, tremendously, never having tried at all. And he realized with absolute clarity that that regret would haunt him every day.

Once he'd framed the choice that way for himself, it was extremely easy for him to make the decision to go ahead with his "crazy" idea. Projecting himself forward into the future, to consider not just the choice but the possible long-term consequences, cleared away the short-term mental clutter and inner conflict that had been holding him back. For instance, he'd been wondering if he should wait till the end of the year before quitting his job so he could earn his annual bonus. (He quit mid-year.)

Considering future regrets is such a simple yet brilliant exercise, and one every would-be entrepreneur should undertake. And it's important to point out that when considering long-term consequences, Bezos didn't think about the bottom line. He didn't question which course of action would make him richer or more famous or would result in greater bragging rights. He considered the *emotional* consequences and concluded he'd be happier and feel more fulfilled and, frankly, more proud of himself if he knew that at least he'd tried.

* * *

Jeff Bezos's conclusion is one I relate to. Although I didn't call it the Regret Minimization Framework, I considered my options in a similar way and came to the same conclusion about making the break and becoming an entrepreneur. My father taught me to evaluate any major decision by carefully considering what might be the absolute worst thing that could happen. I've always considered major decisions this way and often find I'm willing to deal with the worst things that could happen. I would rather risk living with failure than with regret. Having held some pretty low-status jobs while still managing to feel good about myself, I knew that if I bombed as an entrepreneur I could always get a job doing something else. It wasn't my preferred option, of course. But I knew I'd still be able to hold my head up high and feel better than if I'd been too afraid to try to make my mark my own way.

If you have the courage to risk failure, and if what you're really afraid of is risking regret, then it's time to look at how exactly to make the break.

Chapter 5

Entry Strategies

You know you're an entrepreneur, but how, exactly, do you get started with a new venture (or a second? or a third)? What's the best way?

The best way is the way that works best for you. I recognize that sounds like one of those irritatingly cryptic, non-answer answers. But it's true, because several different factors will influence how you get started. First, there's your employment situation. If you're unemployed, and what you're reading seems exciting and sounds like you, then there's no time like the present. While it isn't fun to be let go from a job, the upside is that you no longer have any excuses for why you can't leave, and you're free to get started today. But if, say, you're running the accounts department for a company where you've worked for years, and where your immediate departure would cause turmoil, you may have to wait a few weeks longer than tomorrow. Yes, you have to burn some bridges when you become an entrepreneur, but there's no point in torching a whole company while you're at it. You should exit a role with the same grace and thoughtfulness with which you accepted it.

Your financial situation will also influence how you make the leap. If you're independently wealthy, you're going to have a lot more control over timing than you will if you've got meagre savings and need to drum up investors. But the latter situation isn't necessarily worse, because it forces you to develop a clearly articulated business plan and think things through in a highly detailed fashion. Greg Chamandy, co-founder of Gildan Activewear Inc., believes the systematic approach is, in fact, preferable, and that the initial start-up phase should be slow and methodical. He's a strong proponent of taking all the time you need to craft a thoroughly researched business plan, incorporating as much detail as possible, then vetting and refining it until it's pitch perfect. He likens the process to writing a movie script. But once your plan has crystallized, he says, "there's no turning back." At that point, you have to move like a gazelle, stopping only briefly to revise your strategy when—not if—you hit roadblocks or must rethink assumptions.

The most important determinants are your own personality and emotional needs, which should directly inform the way you strike out for independence. If you're the kind of person who has been known to fall head over heels in love on a first date, you may feel completely comfortable making the leap well before you have every *i* dotted and *t* crossed. However, if you're the type who studies a restaurant menu carefully and confers with the waiter at length before placing your order, you'll probably feel comfortable only if you consider all the angles and get quite a bit of feedback before making your move.

When and how you finally become an entrepreneur isn't

driven solely by practical issues and financial considerations, nor should it be. Your business is an extension of your personality, and aside from anything else it's an attempt to satisfy your emotional needs in a way that, to date, a traditional job simply has not been able to. When you think about it, you're embarking on a new relationship: you're looking to fall in love with your work. So how you get started, and when you think you're ready, depends very much on who you are and what you need to feel happy and comfortable.

The Disciplined, Orderly Approach

Yung Wu, the 53-year-old managing director of NFQ Ventures, a venture accelerator that funds and provides hands-on mentorship to technology companies with global growth potential, learned self-reliance early in life. Born in Taiwan, he was only five years old when his family arrived in Montreal. Yung didn't speak English or French, and his position as an outsider was further solidified by the fact that his was the only visible minority family on the block. He soon figured out that survival depended on being able to "outrun, outfight, and outsmart" the other kids.

His parents thought he should study medicine. Yung, however, had other ideas: he wanted to go to business school. However, even after he had his MBA, he didn't feel prepared to launch his own business. He thought there were so many more things he'd need to understand and know how to do. So after graduation, he accepted an offer to join Ontario Hydro's management-training program.

It was his first taste of bureaucracy, and it wasn't to his liking. In his opinion, management didn't necessarily implement the best ideas but favoured the ones that got the broadest buy-in and therefore involved the least risk for the top brass. If an idea worked, everyone could share the credit; if it failed, well, hey, it wasn't any one person's fault. Yung also came to the conclusion that rapid progression depended less on talent and the ability to get results than on political savvy. People with sharp elbows seemed to climb the career ladder faster than those with sharp minds. Now, Yung is scrappy and willing to stand his ground—he'd proven that as a child, growing up in Montreal. But he didn't have any interest in spending the next 35 years of his life "fighting and clawing my way up so I could retire with a pension," he says today.

It turned out to be a moot point because within the year, Ontario Hydro downsized and Yung was let go. To him, it seemed that the best and brightest were sent packing while those with longer tenure and political connections were kept on. From this experience, Yung learned two important things: a corporate job no longer guaranteed security; and he never again wanted to work in a situation that he couldn't control. But he still had to acquire the skills he would need to create his own opportunities. So he devised a plan that would allow him to do that. "I basically put together my own training program," he explains. "The idea was that after an eight-year tour of duty with various organizations, I'd be ready to go out on my own."

Yung's next employers ranged from Ontario's Ministry of Transportation, to a top Toronto technology-consulting firm, to Texas Instruments, the software company in Dallas. He never spent more than 18 months in one place (despite being offered promotions if he would stay), and he was never let go from a job again. And along the way, he made a point of identifying and then mastering the skills he'd need as an entrepreneur: how to cold-call potential

clients, develop and close new business, maintain customer relationships, and hire and manage people.

The technology industry underwent dramatic changes during the 1980s; by decade's end, Yung spotted a hotbed of opportunity in a niche of the business software market. The computer
software systems of large institutions like banks and insurance
companies had become albatrosses—outdated and inefficient, yet
staggeringly expensive to replace. Eight years in the corporate sector had given Yung the skills to analyze and solve these kinds of
problems. What if he created a SWAT team of software developers
armed with the latest tools and cutting-edge expertise, built the
fastest and most efficient enterprise software factory in the world,
and went after legacy installations like Air Canada, the Bank of
Canada, and Confederation Life?

In 1990, at the age of 30, Yung left Texas Instruments. By that
point, he was earning about $150,000 a year in a high-prestige
job that involved international travel. He had significant personal
financial responsibilities, too, including a mortgage and a car.
And, to up the ante, the economy was in recession at the time.
Nevertheless, he gave notice at his job, borrowed $10,000 on his
credit cards, purchased a laptop and a fax machine, and, with a
partner, hung out a shingle for Castek Software Factory Inc.

I find Yung's story fascinating, partly because his style is so
different from my own. He is methodical and a planner whereas
I'm more strongly compelled by gut instinct, and the way we each
made the leap to entrepreneurship reflects our differences. It
would be hard to argue with his methods, though. His company
grew exponentially: by year six, it had a staff of 150; the company
he started with just $10,000 now generated approximately $20
million in sales. By 2002, the company employed 400 people and

US sales reached $78 million. Castek did experience a dramatic downturn in its fortunes post 9/11 (you'll hear more in Chapter 8 about how the crisis prompted Yung's profound emotional reckoning), but in 2007, he successfully engineered the company's sale to Oracle.

Easing into It

Let's say you're 27 years old and have what might be considered the world's most enviable job: you work at Google. Let's say that you've also worked in a start-up, become a manager, bought a house and a car, run a marathon, and published a book. A lot of your friends are starting to get married and have babies, but you don't see yourself going down that road. Not yet, anyway. You're distracted by the little voice in your head, which is getting louder every month. It's telling you to give it all up and go out on your own.

Okay, you're thinking, this scenario is clearly fictional. What kind of person gives up a job at Google?!

Jenny Blake. In 2011, after five years with the company, that's exactly what she did. She made her decision during the sabbatical she took to write a book. And then, on her blog, lifeaftercollege. org, she explained why, exactly, she'd decided to walk away "from a six-figure salary, three meals a day, yoga classes, gym, the best health care money can buy, and 25,000 brilliant co-workers to see if [she could] hack it as a solopreneur."

It wasn't that she hated her job. On the contrary. Blake wrote on her blog that she really liked working on the training and career development teams at Google. But she was having "a full-blown love affair" with the sideline she'd started six years before: Jenny Blake Enterprises, her publishing, blogging, coaching, and speaking company. First she'd launched a website and then the blog, and she'd been working on them nights and weekends ever since. She was bubbling over with ideas about how to develop the various arms of her company, but realized she couldn't possibly invest emotionally in both her day job *and* her own company. When she was first moonlighting, it wasn't a huge problem because her company and ambitions were relatively small. But now that both had grown, she worried about shortchanging her team at Google. And she worried about shortchanging her readers—and herself— too. During her sabbatical she vacillated every day about what to do, and spent the three months living in limbo.

Like anyone contemplating going it alone, Blake was "slightly terrified" about how she was going to feed herself. But she'd already proven herself to be fairly adept at scaring up income based on her talent, so that wasn't her main concern. What really struck terror into her heart was the prospect of losing the currency that came with having a dream gig at a company widely viewed to be one of the coolest, most innovative in the world—one where thousands applied and were rejected every day. Talk about street cred. If she walked into a party and told people she worked at Google, their eyes lit up because, automatically, they assumed she was smart, interesting, and successful. If she quit, she'd lose that badge of identity. It turned out that her job didn't feed her just literally, but figuratively, too: it fed her ego. The thought of having to relinquish what was in effect an internationally recognized seal of approval of her worth was emotionally destabilizing.

In the end, she had to admit to herself that she'd felt "lighter, freer, and happier" during her sabbatical than at any other time in her life. Feeling like that was, ultimately, worth more to her even than a good job at a company with a great pedigree. At Google, she was set for life—but even though it was a good life, she wanted one that was even better. So she swallowed hard and decided to take her own advice about living large, by leaving "all of the perks behind for the uncertain promise of a more passionate future."

And once she decided, she knew unequivocally that she'd made the right decision. "There is a part of me that deeply trusts that things will work out," she wrote, "*and* another part of me that knows I will have to work my *ass* off to meet the universe halfway."

Pushed into It

You've probably heard of Bernie Marcus and Arthur Blank, co-founders of The Home Depot. What you may not know is what prompted them to launch their business. As reported in *Entrepreneur*, back in the 1970s, Marcus and Blank worked for a home-improvement chain in Southern California called Handy Dan, as CEO and VP of finance, respectively. When a corporate fixer notorious for decimating senior management arrived on the scene to turn around Daylin Inc., Handy Dan's troubled parent company, Marcus and Blank figured their jobs were safe: after all, Handy Dan was making tons of money. They figured wrong. In 1978, the pair was summarily fired.

But getting fired, it turned out, was the best thing that could possibly have happened to them. It provided them with the kick in the pants they needed to change course and provided their catapult to independence. Getting the boot as a precursor to entrepreneurial fame and fortune is, it turns out, a common theme: many wildly successful entrepreneurs were tossed from jobs before they found their calling. Walt Disney was fired from the *Kansas City Star*: his editor told the young cartoonist that he wasn't creative enough. Author J. K. Rowling was sacked from her secretarial job at Amnesty International's London office because she daydreamed too much and secretly wrote stories on her work computer.

Initially, however, getting the axe usually seems catastrophic, even to the most independent-minded people in the world. Very few people heave a sigh of relief and say, "Thank God, now I can focus on starting my own business!" Most wring their hands and wonder how they're going to put food on the table. That thought certainly occurred to Marcus and Blank. When they were let go, the downside was glaringly evident: they were unemployed and broke—and Marcus was, at 49, not exactly a spring chicken. The upside, however, was that both of them had decades of experience in the field, and a track record of making money for other companies. Getting fired had a way of focusing them. They realized they were tired of working for others and doing a good job yet still being viewed as expendable. They believed they could harness their talents and skills to build a company—and some equity—of their own.

As it turned out, before being turfed the two executives had been test-driving an idea in one of the Handy Dan stores. They had discovered that when they discounted products, the volume of sales increased. They'd been planning to see how their experiment worked across the whole chain of stores, but after they were fired decided to find some way to implement their core insight and run with it themselves.

They started meeting regularly at a coffee shop to hammer out a business plan. That's when they discovered that quite apart from providing excellent motivation to go into business for themselves, getting brutally tossed from a company they'd helped build had a way of honing their killer instincts. It revved up their desire to compete, and that in turn proved to be a clarifying force when they were developing a retail strategy of their own. As they batted about ideas, they returned to one nagging question over and over: What unique combination of features do we need so that we can beat Handy Dan?

Out of those meetings came the vision to create a chain of big-box stores with a huge product selection at low prices, and the idea of staffing the stores with highly trained personnel who could answer customers' questions instead of just operating the cash register. The high-concept pitch was to combine the service and convenience of a local hardware store with the selection and discounted prices only a warehouse outlet can offer.

They found investors in New York and in June 1979 opened their first store in suburban Atlanta. But because the full-page ad they'd placed in the newspaper to announce their grand opening never ran, opening day was a bust. Marcus likes to tell the story of how they gave their kids one-dollar bills and had them stand at the store exit to hand out to customers as a thank-you gift for shopping at the store. They figured they'd run out of bills by noon, but by the end of the day the kids were in the parking lot trying to entice people *into* the store with one-dollar bribes. They literally couldn't give the money away. Marcus was so depressed that for a while his wife wouldn't let him handle a razor. He and Blank pressed on, though, and by its second year their company was in the black. Expansion was steady and solid: in 1989, Home Depot opened its hundredth store. Today, it's the largest home-improvement specialty retailer in the world.

And Handy Dan? Well, that chain also passed a major milestone in 1989. It folded.

Falling into It

Samantha Reynolds, president and founder of Echo Memoirs, a Vancouver-based company that produces corporate histories and personal biographies in the form of beautifully written and designed coffee-table books, didn't grow up yearning to run her own business. Now, she had a great role model: her mother, a single mom who owned an antique shop and took Samantha to garage sales, to treasure hunt, on weekends. But Samantha never really thought of herself as an entrepreneur. She was more the creative type who loved to write, and she had an eye for design and visual presentation.

After graduating from university, she freelanced as a writer and desktop publisher for a couple of years, but then an event in her personal life changed her trajectory altogether: her grandmother lost her memory after a routine hip operation. Samantha was devastated; all the family stories had been lost, forever. Her reaction was to begin recording the life histories of other family members and friends. They responded so enthusiastically to the idea that she recognized she'd stumbled onto a business opportunity. So in 1999, at the age of 24, she launched a one-woman memoir-writing business out of her home. To develop a portfolio, she put together the first few books for free.

Samantha didn't have Yung Wu's carefully collected business know-how, but psychologically and emotionally she was extremely well prepared—by circumstances, not design. Without even having to try, she'd intuitively picked up how her entrepreneurial mother dealt with the challenges of the lifestyle. And as Samantha points out, she was an only child, so she didn't learn the art of compromise at an early age. This might have been a problem when she was in kindergarten and unaccustomed to sharing her crayons, but it prepared her well for autonomy. Self-reliance was already her default command. Not only was she unaccustomed to consulting with others before making decisions; she didn't like having to do so. She much preferred making up her own mind and going after what she wanted without hesitation or waiting for someone else to agree to come along.

Coming of age in the dot-com era also set her up well, not just financially but psychologically. She'd been paid handsomely at a young age, so by the time she was 24, she'd saved enough to sustain herself for a good half-year. She distinctly remembers thinking very pragmatically about her options and deciding, "Hey, I'm young. I don't have a mortgage or kids, so if there's ever a time to throw some savings at an idea and see if it works, this is it." She reasoned that if she blew her savings, well, so what? She had a whole lifetime to earn it back. And because she had been earning a good amount of money to date, she figured that if the whole memoir thing didn't pan out, she'd just figure out another way to leverage her talents—go back to freelancing, or maybe even get hired somewhere.

The idea of launching a start-up didn't scare her because in the dot-com world it was the new cool thing to do and there were young millionaires all over the place. And because she'd already freelanced, she didn't have to adjust to the idea of independence the way Yung or the Home Depot guys did. It wasn't really all that different from what she'd already been doing. What she had to get comfortable with was the risk of putting more resources into selling and marketing her own talent.

Samantha hadn't taken any business classes at university, but she does remember thinking when she was starting out that there was something odd about investors pouring millions of dollars into dot-com start-ups without any sense of when they might begin to see a return on their investment. "I told myself, *I guess these smart people just know more than I do,*" she remembers. "But when the boom went bust, I had the sense that my instincts weren't so off, and that fortified my confidence that I didn't need an MBA to start a company," she adds. (Having a front-row seat for the boom-and-bust drama also emboldened her to rely on a really simple business model: make more money than you spend.)

But perhaps the real learning from the dot-com years, which she says "permanently scarred me—in a good way," was the notion that anyone could start with a dream and transform it into a reality. During that time, she also picked up another belief system— one that she holds deeply to this day—centred around the idea that "work could be outrageously enjoyable." She says, "It was the age of pool tables at the office. Even if I couldn't afford that, I felt entitled to a blurring of joy from my personal life to my work life, to do work I loved and live a lifestyle I loved. That imprinted on me during those dot-com years, so I didn't feel pressured to take a boring old job."

Not that starting her own business was always a cakewalk. "At the beginning, I thought, *Well, no biggie if this doesn't work out.* But then I fell madly in love with the company I was building. Not just the idea—I found the thrill of building it totally addictive. And I realized, *I have to make this work. It can't fail.* Even though it almost did fail so many times. I still remember going to buy groceries with my fingers crossed that there'd be enough money in my bank account. And when my card was rejected, I'd say, 'Oh, I don't know why that happened,' and I'd put aside the grapes and papayas because they were more expensive."

Monitoring her fruit intake must have worked wonders

because in year three Samantha moved the business out of her home and into a beautiful studio space in a heritage building. (In the fall of 2012, the company relocated again, after a fire in the building.) In 14 years, Echo Memoirs has grown gradually but steadily. Today, it has six full-time employees and 19 freelance contractors; produces 12–15 projects a year for clients across North America, including lululemon, The North West Company, and Goldcorp; and generates multi-millions in revenue.

But two things haven't changed for Samantha since the early days. First, she still finds making compromises "a little bit tedious. You can ask my husband. Even my team has to politely remind me that they like to be consulted. It's not natural to me." And the second constant? "The simplicity and thrill of autonomy."

* * *

How will *you* know when you're finally ready to implement your own entry strategy? If you're a disciplined, orderly person like Yung Wu, you'll probably want to spend a few months—or, as in Yung Wu's case, a few years—honing your skills and methodically planning your leap to entrepreneurship. Just remember that no plan is bulletproof. No matter how well thought out your entry plan is, you are about to step into a new, constantly changing reality. If planning it out helps you take the step, then by all means plan away. Just know your plan may be out of date the minute it collides with reality.

Maybe, like Samantha Reynolds, you find that your life has presented you with an opportunity to launch a business doing something you love and you're young enough and free enough to take the risk without having to think too hard about it. (Oh, to return to those days.) The bottom line is that the way you get started as an entrepreneur is entirely up to you. Your choices for how to do it are endless. But if you allow yourself to get caught up trying to do it perfectly, your brilliant business may *never* get off the ground.

The thing about taking a leap of faith is that you're jumping into the unknown. There's no possible way to feel 100 percent ready. So if you wait until you are, you'll never get started. At some point you just have to hold your nose, jump off the diving board, and trust that you'll figure things out on the way down. How do you know your time is drawing near? You start to notice your desire for independence is beginning to dominate and direct your thinking. You wake up one day and realize you're already starting to mentally let go of the sure thing. You're beginning to feel excited that your life is your own to live.

Chapter 6

Going It Alone

For some people, the lifestyle challenges associated with entrepreneurship—the psychological and emotional adjustments, the relationship challenges—start the moment they decide to become independent. For others, the changes will take a little longer to show up. Either way, once you bite the bullet and make the leap to entrepreneurship or decide to take up the challenge again, your life will change—and continue to change—in unexpected ways. Handling these changes means preparing the people you love for the all-in lifestyle.

Unfortunately, many entrepreneurs are simply too busy and too distracted to ask how the entrepreneurial lifestyle will impact them until they find themselves in the deep end of the pool. Some start swimming right away, while others tread water for a bit, scanning the horizon for a lifeguard or at least a swim coach. But some flounder, then sink, dragged down by "personal" issues they never thought would interfere with their ability to start a business.

How well you adjust to independence depends a great deal on

your temperament, stamina, and flexibility. And how well those *around* you adjust to your independence depends a great deal on their expectations, your self-awareness, everyone's communication skills—and, frankly, just how saintly and tolerant they are. Both you and the people you love will need to prepare to live through huge and unexpected challenges that will come at *the worst* times.

You can't really know what it's like to be an entrepreneur until you've actually become one. And your significant other won't have a clue what it's like to live with an entrepreneur until he or she has signed on for the ride. About all you can do is try to anticipate and prepare for the emotional challenges you're likely to face as meticulously as you rehearsed for the business challenges.

And how, exactly, do you do that? Well, first by recognizing that emotional obstacles come with the territory and you'll have to get over them just as you'll have to leap business hurdles. And second, by recognizing that you should take the emotional challenges every bit as seriously.

Battling Self-Doubt

Here's the good news: in the first blush of independence, the feeling you're most likely to experience is exhilaration. You're free! You've left limbo behind and can now devote your time and energy to creating something that you care passionately about and which is also a consummate reflection of you: your values, your skills, your personality. You'll be on a total high, feeling more energized than you have in years, and discover that what everybody told you is true: you can hardly wait to get to work in the morning. The only thing you'll regret is that you took so long to make the leap.

If you'd known how amazing you were going to feel, you wouldn't have wasted a minute waffling.

But sooner or later, it will hit you: you're all in all right—and you're also all alone. Everything depends on you. *You're it.* That realization will usually be followed by a sickening wave of self-doubt, and that's because entrepreneurs are only human. We often have the expectations (and livelihoods) of dozens of employees, lenders, and investors tied up in our ability to make the right choices. When this awareness hits you—little old you—you'll start questioning your abilities and wondering if you've made a terrible mistake. On good days during the start-up phase, you'll have this debate with yourself once a day. On bad days, it will start as soon as you wake up and still be raging as you fall asleep.

You're not an idiot. Of course, you understood that being an entrepreneur means going it alone. That's one reason it was such a tough decision. But back then, your knowledge of what independence would feel like on a daily basis was purely theoretical. To some extent, it was almost certainly influenced by media reports on successful entrepreneurs, who made independence look pretty appealing. Intellectually, you understood what you were getting into, or thought you did. But now you comprehend on an emotional level what it really means to fly without a net. And that moment of truth may have opened a Pandora's box full of insecurities.

When I first started out, most of the time I managed to leave others with the impression that I knew what I was talking about. On the inside, however, I was frequently a basket case. On many days, my emotions ricocheted between two opposite poles. On the one hand, I was brimming with messianic zeal and confidence about what I had to offer the world of marketing. On the other, I was riddled with uncertainty about my worth and abilities. Here's a sampling of the running internal debate that played on an endless loop in my head:

> *I can do this. I know I can.*
> *Oh God, I can't do this. What was I thinking?*
> *I'm not sure I'm doing this right. I'm going to fall flat on my face and be humiliated. Everyone will find out I'm a fraud.*
> *Stop whining! You have to do this. You will do this. Maybe.*

Somehow, I'd managed to land a marketing job with nothing but a high school education. Suddenly, I found myself advising CEOs on how to take their products to the marketplace. I lived in constant fear that somebody would find out I'd slipped through the door by mistake. They'd stand up in one of those meetings and say, "Who the hell are *you* to be telling me this?"

Through sheer force of will (and, okay, the need to put food on the table) I survived those moments of self-doubt and managed to deliver a passable imitation of a confident professional. But often, afterward, I couldn't believe that I'd pulled it off, and was a little shocked that I hadn't been shown the door. I battle my self-doubts by compartmentalizing—I'll tell you later exactly how I do this.

Feeling Afraid, Stressed, Overwhelmed—and Going Ahead Anyway

Now, maybe you have a great idea and can sell it with the confidence and showmanship of Tony Robbins. But when you're starting out on a new venture, you don't know what you don't know, and this will become readily apparent, even to you. At least some of the time you'll be so far out of your comfort zone that the only way you can go forward is by striding purposefully into situations you'd rather shrink away from. Hence, the ongoing internal battle where one voice is lecturing you and shoving you out of the plane, and the other is heckling and predicting your parachute won't open.

Shane Skillen is no stranger to the internal tug-of-war between confidence and self-doubt. He was 24 years old and the founder of a then little-known market research firm, Hotspex, when he started booking meetings with potential clients who had never heard of him or the cutting-edge customer-insight tools he was pitching. He had unwavering faith in his company. Yet, when it came to his ability to woo a prospective client? Not so much. Shane was horribly afraid of presenting and turned bright red when he spoke in public. "I would have preferred death by lethal injection over presenting to even two people." And while fear of public speaking is common, it can be the kiss of death for a new entrepreneur. In Shane's case, his inability to shut off his self-doubt and present effectively was "seriously limiting" his ability to build his business. "I was terrified I would let my partners and investors down by not being able to bring on clients," he says.

Rather than face up to his fears—by scheduling even more presentations in order to give himself a chance to practise—Shane opted for a state-of-the-art surgical procedure that would stop the blushing. The surgery worked. Shane was able to handle meetings without turning bright red, and the result gave him a short-term boost in confidence . . . until he discovered a debilitating side effect: compensatory sweating. "They should have called it, 'You will sweat through four thick cotton T-shirts even when it is just slightly above room temperature.'" Shane discovered the side effect one afternoon while having lunch with a prospective client. They were sitting on a patio, enjoying their meals, when Shane noticed his lunch partner staring at him strangely. "I looked as if somebody had shot me with a water gun from my chest down." He finished his meeting and immediately booked himself to have the surgery reversed. When he recovered, he got over his fear of pitching the old-fashioned way: with time, practice, and advice from mentors.

I love Shane's story because it illustrates a really important lesson about overcoming self-doubt: you can't sidestep it or shortchange it. Self-doubt isn't going anywhere. You have to make your way through it patiently and train yourself to function right along with it. The best way to do this is to remind yourself of all the times you've felt the fear and done what you needed to do anyway. For instance, Shane didn't cut short his meeting because he had sweated through his shirt. He kept going in spite of the fear and embarrassment. Today, when he looks back on the experience, he can laugh it off. But more importantly, he can look at it as proof that he's been capable of trumping self-doubt for the sake of progress. Does Shane still suffer from nerves and uncertainty? Hell, yes. We all do. But for Shane—and for countless other entrepreneurs, for whom salesmanship and presentations are part of life—the nerves don't usually kick in unless he's on stage in front of a few hundred people.

If you've left a company, you'd better steel yourself for more ego-battering. People thought Jenny Blake was crazy when she said goodbye to a career at Google and went out on her own, but the experience holds true even if you leave a company that has far less sex appeal. You've cut your ties to the mother ship, but you haven't yet built up any credibility of your own. With no corporate badge to flash so others can easily peg you and decide whether you're interesting or valuable enough to warrant their attention, you'll find that you excite a lot less interest. You'll introduce yourself, and people will go, "Huh?"

When that happens—and it will happen—it's pretty awful. You feel like a flea on a gnat's back. And it's incredibly hard to keep driving forward when you feel so puny. But as emotionally disoriented as you feel at such moments, you have to swallow hard and continue to drive forward because each new person you meet is an opportunity to convert a no to a yes. Expect to encounter a hundred no's or half-hearted maybe's before you get to a yes. If it feels like a little death every time you announce yourself to a person whose eyes promptly glaze over, you'll never get there.

The other day I realized that the debate I used to have with myself when I first started my business is similar to the one I still have with myself four mornings a week, when I'm supposed to go jogging. Not a morning goes by that I don't lie in bed making bargains with myself to try to get out of running. I can be extremely resourceful when the occasion demands it, so I always manage to come up with a long list of reasons why I'm fully entitled to pull the covers over my head and hit the snooze button. Ultimately, however, what gets my feet on the floor is reminding myself that if I don't do my workout, nobody else will do it for me. I'm the only person responsible for how I'm going to feel about myself, and how much physical energy I'm going to have later in the day if I don't run (read: not a whole lot). If I go several days without exercising and feel poorly because of it, I have only myself to blame. I chose independence because I wanted to be in control of my life, and that means taking full responsibility for it in every sense: professionally, physically, financially, emotionally.

I don't want to exaggerate and pretend that, early on, your sense of self-doubt is so crushing that you can barely stagger through the day. You'll have great days when you're buoyed by self-confidence. And with time and experience, self-doubt does ease somewhat, and it also becomes easier to quash it when it does arise, because you have more ammunition in your arsenal: you remind yourself of the good results you've had; and of the times you were scared out of your mind but persisted anyway, and the irrefutable fact that your business is still alive and kicking, which means you must not be completely clueless. It's a virtuous circle: the more you put yourself out there, the more confidence you develop. And once you learn to manage your insecurities, the faster you'll rebound when they resurface next time.

But unless you're a raging egomaniac, nagging self-doubt never vanishes altogether. It's always lurking in a dark corner of your psyche, ready to pounce, no matter how successful you are.

Dave Buckle, the Funk-Off founder who walked off the street and into a *Dragons' Den* audition more or less on impulse, comes off as a supremely confident guy, especially when he's talking about the all-natural deodorant he invented. And yet, he too has moments when doubt shakes him to his core. After Dave was on the show and persuaded me to do the due diligence around investing in his company, my CFO and I met with him and his partner, as is standard procedure when reviewing an investment. We need to see facts, figures, and some solid proof that what we've been sold is as solid as we perceived from the first presentation. Dave had a good feeling about the meeting and thought it had gone well. But when the phone still hadn't rung a few weeks later, he began to second-guess himself: "Holy crap. Did I blow it? Did I act too familiar? I thought I made an emotional connection but maybe I was too relaxed—too much myself? Maybe I should have been more proper?" He needn't have worried—he was great in the meeting. And although we opted not to invest because of the early stage of the opportunity, I have no doubt he will do well.

Talking about all this later, Dave explained, "When you work for yourself, you have the luxury of remaining true to your instincts. You can't freewheel it like that if you're representing someone else. But the flip side of that freedom is that you really have to put yourself out there, and sometimes that can be a real emotional roller coaster."

When you're in the hurly-burly of a start-up, you have to devise some armour to protect yourself from your own insecurities. For me, that's meant learning to live with them and accepting that there never will be a moment when they magically disappear and I think, *At last, I've finally arrived.* Even today, I view insecurity as part of the lifestyle. And while it has become less insistent over the years, I think it's never going to go away altogether. I wish I'd known this upfront, because I could have saved myself a lot of self-flagellation. If you're just starting out, it's one thing I really hope you take to heart: self-reliance doesn't necessarily entail self-confidence—and self-confidence is not, in my experience, a 24/7 state. It comes and goes when you're an entrepreneur, and what you need to do is find a way to ride out the lows. Knowing that they're inevitable is a good start.

Boarding the Stress Express

There are very few certainties for entrepreneurs. Stress is one of them. During a start-up, or any period of change or exponential growth, it's one of the few things you can count on: bad things will happen that stress you to the core. Now, maybe you've had stressful jobs before and you've managed just fine, so you're not too worried. Stress is stress is stress, you may be thinking.

Well, you can skip these pages if you like, but before you do, I feel compelled to caution you that the stress you'll encounter as an entrepreneur isn't the same as the kind you deal with when you work for someone else. It is so different that, in fact, it probably deserves a new name all its own, to distinguish it. Why? For one thing, you have way more riding on the outcome, which will feel like a verdict not just on your business but on your identity, because the business is an extension of you. For another, you will have to deal with it completely alone, unable to compare notes with colleagues or, at least initially, to delegate responsibilities so that you can ease your own burden.

What will cause all this stress? Well, perhaps the better question is: What won't? During start-up, the list is long, but let's cut to the chase: your number-one worry will be money. (Like a home renovation, your start-up will cost more and take longer than you thought.)

Even if you thought through potential costs carefully beforehand, and asked trusted advisers to eyeball your projections, and put your numbers through hypothetical stress tests to make sure they'd hold up under pressure, a financial crisis will come as surely as the sun will rise tomorrow. And when it does, it will ride into town with its trusty sidekick: Anxiety. If you don't learn how to lasso Anxiety, tape its mouth shut, and hog-tie it, it might be your undoing.

This crisis will happen whether you're just starting out or you're an established entrepreneur. Tanya Shaw was well into her entrepreneurial life when a major financial setback threatened to sabotage the custom-fit body-scanning business that she'd spent more than a decade building.

The Halifax native started her first business, a custom-sewing company, when she was still in university. At 19 she bought a house (the mortgage was co-signed by her parents), rented out the basement, lived in the back, and set up fitting rooms and sewing stations for two seamstresses in the front. Over the next few years, she built up a list of close to 500 clients in the Halifax area—mostly professional women, many of whom complained about how difficult it was to find clothes that fit them perfectly. So Tanya bought patterns and redrew the lines in order to create properly fitting clothes for her clients. But it was time-consuming, so she started to look for opportunities to automate custom-pattern creation.

A few years after graduating from university, she launched a special software designed to create custom patterns based on body measurement data. Over time, this idea morphed into early plans for Me-Ality, a state-of-the-art body scanner designed to take a person's measurements and provide a list of perfectly fitting clothes from a list of major retailers. To build the scanner, Tanya would need capital—and a lot of it. So in 2002, shortly after she discovered she was pregnant, she began one of her first major drives to raise venture capital. She signed a deal with an institutional investor, which stipulated that the money would be delivered in two stages. The investor also asked that Tanya speed up development of the technology as much as possible. The day she gave birth to her daughter, she also got some bad news: the investor group had decided to pull her second round of funding, a move that left the new mother with enormous bills and no money to pay them.

"It was awful on every level," Tanya says. "I felt nobody understood what I was going through, and I didn't think anyone could help me." The anxiety was worse than anything she'd ever experienced, but if she had let it get to her she might have been incapacitated. Instead, she consciously ignored her panicky thoughts and carefully reviewed her options. Her choices were to try to fight the investors into releasing the money or to find the cash elsewhere. And while their decision to hold back the money galled her, she didn't think she had the energy or stamina to grow her business, care for her baby, and fight a legal battle. Instead, she invited her senior team to her Halifax home to brainstorm potential solutions. Within weeks, she had found a number of angel investors to provide short-term capital, and a year later she signed a new financing deal with terms that were more favourable than the first. Today, the scanner, Me-Ality, is in more than 70 US malls and provides sizing on more than 150 brands. In 2011, Tanya completed one of the largest raises of private venture capital in Canadian history.

Now, let's take a look at another scenario. Say you worked intensely on your business model for months, launched your business, and then discovered you'd made a serious mathematical error—serious enough that you had to go to your charter customers and tell them they needed to pony up a lot more cash. How high do you think your anxiety level would be then?

This isn't a hypothetical situation. It's exactly what happened to Zipcar founder Robin Chase. A few months into her start-up, as reported in *Inc.*, she realized to her horror that the daily rental rates she'd promised to the company's 400-and-counting members were way too low, and if she didn't raise them, her company would fail. Yet barely out of the starting gate, and only weeks away from closing a major funding deal, she was understandably terrified of irreparably damaging her reputation with customers and investors. On the evening she discovered her error, Chase cried for two hours straight. Then she got a grip and sent customers an email telling them straight out that she'd screwed up and would have to raise the rates she'd promised.

Imagine being in Chase's shoes that night. How much sleep do you think you'd get? How much dread do you think you'd feel checking your email inbox the next morning? Would you even have the courage? As it turns out, her story had a happy ending: the majority of her customers were understanding. Not ecstatic about the bad news, of course, but not vowing to destroy the company, either. Two did fire off angry letters, but she called them both personally and talked them around. Remarkably, in the end, none of Zipcar's charter clients left. But, of course, Robin Chase didn't know that would be the outcome. I think it's safe to say that you'd need nerves of steel to make it through the Olympian level of stress she endured.

Thankfully, you can develop nerves of steel on the job. CNN's chief international correspondent, Christiane Amanpour, who reports from the world's most dangerous war zones, told PBS that, while people routinely call her "fearless," she doesn't think anyone is without fear. It's all about how well you manage your fears. I completely agree with her. And the best way I've ever found to manage my fears is by compartmentalizing them.

If you ask me, compartmentalization has gotten a bad rap. A lot of people view it as a shortcoming, as though a truly evolved person has no need to box anything off. Personally, I think it's a necessary skill for all entrepreneurs. I know for sure that I wouldn't have been able to handle the pressures of my lifestyle if I lacked the ability to wall off feelings that threatened to derail me emotionally or to throw me off my game professionally. All of us have theories about ourselves, and one of mine is that I developed the ability to compartmentalize early in life; it was a survival skill I needed, growing up in a family where I had to learn to shut out the noise. If I had dwelled on what was bothering me, my feelings would have overwhelmed me. Instead, I figured out how to set them aside in another part of my brain, where they couldn't hurt or bother me.

That adaptive mechanism from my childhood has turned out to be one of my biggest assets, professionally speaking. Compartmentalization has helped me deal much more effectively with panic and stress. I've learned to do—to be productive rather than wring my hands on the sidelines. I manage my worry by isolating my problems and chipping away at them incrementally. And when I'm not chipping, I close the door on them and go do something else.

Think about the problem you're facing and ask yourself if there is a step or a series of actions that you can take today to address it. If there is something you need to do immediately to address your anxiety, by all means go and do it. But if there isn't a clear path of action that you can take today, you need to give yourself permission to temporarily let it go. I do this by thinking: *There's nothing I can do about this now. So I'm moving on.* And every time the fear bubbles up, I'll repeat that mantra. It's a Jedi mind trick, and it works like a charm.

Dividing and conquering emotional reactions in this way

helps me tame my anxiety. It's also helped me to focus on what's important and use my time more efficiently. If you can close the door on your worries, you're much better able to stay in the moment and connect emotionally with others, which is so important both professionally and personally. With my anxiety under control, or at least tucked away for the time being, it's not constantly distracting me when I should be focusing on someone or something else. As long as I know I'll wrestle the problem at some later time—as opposed to procrastinating about dealing with it, or living in denial of its existence (which only increases my stress)—I'm able to keep a leash on my anxieties and function pretty well.

Another trick I've learned, and one I've really come to rely on whenever I have to make an important decision, is to set the problem aside for a while and let it marinate in my subconscious until a solution bubbles up to the surface—which, by the way, it always does. It turns out that there's scientific evidence to back up this idea that our conscious and unconscious minds work in tandem to solve tough problems. A recent Harvard Business School study suggests that our unconscious minds might, in fact, be *better* than our conscious minds at coming up with good solutions to complex problems, particularly when our energy is low. For instance, the study found that, if you review information related to a business problem before you go to sleep, you're likely to think more creatively on the problem the following morning. I buy into this belief because so many times when I've been facing a real dilemma, the answer has come only after I've allowed myself to relax and move on to something else. This process is now second nature for me, but in the beginning I had to train myself to trust my subconscious mind to work it out. Again, this is an instance in which it helps to talk to yourself. You might say something along the lines of *I don't have the answer right now, but it will come to me if I let my mind do its work.* Does it sound a little woo-woo? Possibly. Does it work? Absolutely.

The really interesting news on anxiety, according to one Gallup poll I saw, is that while entrepreneurs are slightly more likely than other workers to experience stress and worry, they're also more optimistic about their future and more likely to report that they experience enjoyment and learn something new each day. Stress may just be the cost of those benefits. We grumble about it, but don't decide the price is so outrageous that we have to chuck the whole entrepreneurial thing.

Stop Expecting People to "Get" You

Ask 10 people whether you should take a risk, and nine will tell you it's a terrible idea. We've already seen what happens the minute you tell somebody you're thinking about going out on your own: the naysayers come out of the woodwork.

Once you actually are independent, you'll have to fend off a whole new subset of people who feel compelled to offer you advice (whether you've solicited it or not) and to critique your choices. Carbon Farmer's Brad Rabiey (with whom I partnered in the business after his appearance on *Dragons' Den*) told me that even though his family has some first-hand knowledge of entrepreneurship—three generations of Rabieys have worked on the family farm—they still ask, "Why are you doing this? Why are you pushing yourself so hard?" And also, "Why don't you and Rebecca produce some grandbabies and hang out with us more?" Brad knows his family is genuinely concerned about how hard he and his wife work, and he also knows that they miss him and would like to spend more time with him. Yet even though they mean well, their comments sometimes still bother him.

People who foist their opinions on you, however, don't always mean well. Some are motivated by jealousy: you took a risk when they couldn't or wouldn't, and your willingness to put yourself out there feels threatening to them. On some level, they may sort of want you to fail, although they may not even be conscious of their motivations. But you will be. It will come through loud and clear in the sharpness of their criticism and their unwillingness to back off. If you feel personally attacked, run, don't walk, in the other direction. These are the most emotionally dangerous people for an entrepreneur whose confidence is already a bit shaky.

Other skeptics truly do have your best interests at heart. However, they tend to offer advice based on their personal experience, which may be a world away from yours, particularly if they've never run a business. When you're grappling with self-doubt, even questioners with good intentions can throw you off.

A case in point: what Natasha Vandenhurk of Three Farmers Camelina Oil experienced when she was expecting her first child. She was due in January 2013, and she planned to take about three weeks off after she had the baby. To prepare, she'd hired someone new to take on some of the day-to-day tasks she'd been managing at the company. Natasha hoped her baby would be a good sleeper, in which case she hoped to continue to work, though much less intensely, between feedings and also in the evenings. Since January and February are generally slower months for the company, and her husband and family had already signed on to pitch in, she felt reasonably confident she'd be able to manage.

Others, however, assured her she would not—and that she

shouldn't even want to. The gist of the predictions was that she would fall madly in love with being at home with an infant, and would drop all this nonsense about getting back to work as soon as possible. "People make assumptions," she says. "They think you're going to react the same way they did." Her maternity leave, she was assured by many, simply wasn't long enough. "Oh, you'll feel differently when the baby comes," they'd chuckle knowingly. Or, "Remember: the baby comes first!"

"They don't understand what I'm trying to juggle," says Natasha, who has a strong emotional attachment to her work. She wasn't fretting about the prospect of leaving the baby at home. She was more concerned about being out of the loop while others attended a hugely important trade show out east.

She tried to limit conversations with know-it-alls by not engaging. "I always keep my answer minimal. I say, 'I'm going to work through it. My life is a bit different from yours.'" However, she wasn't able to ignore the barrage of advice completely. "Internally, maybe I don't manage it that well," she admits. She found herself wondering if perhaps everyone was right and she'd wind up pining to stay home with the baby. But how could she manage that? These kinds of thoughts chased each other's tails in her brain, and she wasn't sure how to shut them down.

"If I have an unknown in my work, I talk to people. I research. Then I execute based on my research," Natasha explains. "But it's different in your personal life."

The Pitfalls of Borrowing from Friends and Family

If you need money to get your business up and running, you will likely try to scare it up wherever you can and may decide to ask family and friends either to invest or to give you a loan. When people ask me how to go about that, I always tell them, "Very carefully."

I understand the temptation. Sometimes you're so desperate for a cash infusion, you start seeing the people around you as piggy banks. They have money. You need money. Ergo, they should fork it over.

On *Dragons' Den*, Kevin O'Leary likes to say that money has no emotions. But what he misses is the point that money is the driver of so *many* emotions. And the degree of emotion people attach to their money ranges from mild to deeply pathological, so you have to be really selective about whom you ask—even if you think investors stand to make a bundle in the long run, and even if your friends are clamouring to invest. I recommend asking yourself a few key questions before approaching family and friends for cash: Is this person in a position to lose whatever she invests? Is she risk-averse by nature? Will I have to hold her hand through the whole ride, and am I willing and able to do that? Will I feel beholden in a way that could destroy the fabric of the relationship? How will I feel if I cause her to lose her life savings? What would a smaller loss, even, do to our friendship, and to my entire social circle?

You may think it's the other person's responsibility to decide whether he can afford the investment. In fact, though, the onus lies on you, too. Let's face it: if your grandmother winds up losing money, you'll be the one who will have to deal with the emotional repercussions, while she has to deal with the stark financial ones. For her, it won't be the same as losing money on a mutual fund. She won't shrug and start singing "Que Sera Sera." She'll be disappointed or distressed or panicky or hopping mad. But more than that, *you* will be devastated. And, oh yeah . . . she's got your phone number.

When you borrow money from friends or family, it's never a clean transaction. Once you cross that line, the relationship is going to change. It may blow up or it may alter only in subtle ways. But in my experience, it *will* shift. My advice is that even if you're desperate, you should listen to your gut: if you feel just a tiny bit nervous or scared about entering into a financial relationship with someone close to you, don't do it. No matter how desperate you are for cash.

Money always comes at a price. When you borrow from the bank, you pay interest. When you borrow from friends and family, the currency is emotional. It's great when you wind up making everybody rich—then you're a hero (though anyone who chose not to invest or wasn't asked to will likely be resentful). But if you burn through your parents' retirement fund and your siblings' inheritance, Christmas dinner could turn out to be a very frosty affair—if you're still invited, that is.

Remember Chris Emery, of OMG Candy? His family lost a lot of money they'd invested in his first business, and the loss created considerable tension. His dad accused him of blowing the money foolishly, and his siblings wondered, *Why did* he *get all that cash?* Chris felt sick about letting his parents down. "You wear a hat as a pure investor—you take a shot and that's the way it is. But the other hat is that they're your parents." (He has since walked his siblings through what happened, and told them his goal is to pay back every penny their parents lost. He says they're "cool with that.")

Chris subsequently launched an advertising business in Edmonton, but that business failed, too. ("I impulsed on it," he explains today.) Once again, his dad had to bail him out—this time to the tune of 40 grand. "He said, 'Here's 40. Pay me back when you can.'" Fortunately his father is in a position to wait a while. From Chris's point of view, these two businesses were his own form of higher education which his parents might well have helped pay for in a university setting. That being said, he still intends to pay his parents back.

Of course, scoring a cash infusion from relatives or friends doesn't have to be a bad experience. There are many entrepreneurs out there who have managed to pull it off successfully. Take Salah Bachir. Shortly after launching *Premiere* magazine, he put together a special issue for the Toronto International Film Festival. He sold a ton of ads, which almost doubled the page count and prompted his printer to demand upfront payment. Salah couldn't find a bank to give him the upfront financing, which meant that the up-sized issue was poised to become a blockbuster flop. That evening, over dinner with friends, Salah shared the experience—including his fears that if he couldn't produce the issue it could sour relations with his advertisers so badly that the magazine might not recover. The next day one of the friends who was at the dinner showed up at Salah's office with a cheque, telling him he had the money set aside anyway and wanted to give it to Salah to help him through a difficult time. When the revenue from the special issue came in, Salah paid his friend back with interest. And the following year, Salah heard through the grapevine that his friend had cashed in some of his investments to help out.

Salah's experience worked because it ticked his most important *When It's Okay to Ask Friends and Family for Money* box: when the investment is a sure thing. In Salah's case, he'd sold the ads and had signed contracts in place. If he hadn't, he may not have accepted the money. "I have great relationships with my friends and never went to anyone unless I was sure I would be able to easily pay them back," he says. When it comes to approaching friends for money, it's worth remembering that, yes, the people who love you could be a source of much-needed capital. But they'll make a far greater contribution in terms of the moral support they can offer.

What Do You Mean, You Think I'm Blind and Selfish?

In start-up mode, people often behave toward their nearest and dearest in ways they wouldn't normally dream of behaving. If they had any objectivity—which they don't—they'd recognize they'd be appalled if someone else treated them that way. A start-up is as all-consuming as the beginning of an epic love affair, and in a sense that's exactly what it is. You are falling in love with your company. Unfortunately, to others it often appears that what you're obsessed with is yourself.

When you're in start-up mode and work beckons, which it always does, you think nothing of bolting from a family reunion or repeatedly cancelling date night. Your best friend's son's bar mitzvah? You'll send a cheque (and hope it doesn't bounce). Perhaps you have some vague awareness that what you're doing is out of line, but you just don't think the normal rules of social engagement apply to you. *I'm starting a business, for goodness' sake! I don't have time for social niceties.* If you're not careful, though, some key relationships will go right out the window along with your social graces.

The issue is not that you've turned into a sociopath who couldn't care less about other people. It's that you're so consumed with what you're doing, and it's so important to you, that you just

expect others to understand and empathize. When finally someone blows up and yells, "How can you be so self-absorbed? Don't
you care about anyone except yourself?" you will look at him as
though he's speaking Swahili. *What's with you? I'm not an egomaniac! This isn't about* me—*it's about the business!*

During the start-up phase, it's pretty easy to get all puffed up
with your own self-importance. Yes, your business is the biggest
thing going on in your life, but it's not the most important thing
in everybody else's, and they're probably sick and tired of hearing
you go on about it. Face it: you're starting a business, not curing
cancer.

I remember clearly when I got called on the carpet for this
exact sort of behaviour, although it took me quite a few repeat
visits before I even clued in to how insufferable I was being. It was
during a period when I was married to the man I'd promoted—
against my gut instincts—to running my company. At the time,
my four kids were also working with me in and out of the office,
so at dinner we'd talk business. I was, of course, anxious about
the state of business, so it was even more a topic of discussion.
I generally kicked off the conversation, eager to dissect the day's
events and talk about what was next on the agenda. I treated the
business as the centrepiece not just of dinner-table conversation
but of our life as a family.

On several occasions, my eldest daughter told me that I had to
stop doing this. I didn't really understand what she was on about.
I mean, the kids knew about the business, they were working in
it part-time, they could see what an all-consuming endeavour it
was. Well, it turned out, yes, they could. And that's partly why they
yearned for a discussion about anything but the business.

Now, I confess that it took me a while to grasp this fact. I might even have become quite upset when my daughter kept pointing out that I needed to stop talking business. I honestly didn't get it: my kids felt they were unimportant to me. I thought I was showing them respect talking to them about adult matters, sharing my concerns, and looking for their insights. I thought I was making them feel valued. But to them it seemed as if I considered the business more important than anything—including my kids.

It took me a long time, probably far too long, to understand that my family didn't want to live the business 24/7, as I did. Today, I really work hard not to bring up business when I'm with them, especially on holidays. (Okay, I'll confess that part of my motivation here is selfish, as they've threatened repeatedly to toss my BlackBerry into the ocean.) Funnily enough, now that my kids are adults and even more involved in the business, when the conversation heads in that direction, more often than not I'm the one who shuts it down. It took me a while, but I did take the lesson to heart. Simply because you're all in on your business does not mean it's the only topic of interest you should discuss. Being rounded as a person is the best gift you can give to yourself, to your family, and to your business.

* * *

People think of entrepreneurs as big risk-takers, and it's true that we're more comfortable with risk than the average person is. But by and large, we're not partial to crazy risks like going to Vegas and dropping a bundle on a lucky number. We much prefer calculated risks, where we feel we have some control over the outcome.

The good news is that if you anticipate the emotional and psychological hazards ahead, you will have some control. You can adjust accordingly to avoid some dangers altogether and minimize the impact of others. But as with the financial aspects of a business, you need to do your due diligence in order to have any hope of controlling the outcome. Have an honest conversation with yourself and those close to you about what to expect, and keep that conversation going as your business moves from dream to reality. If you're at all like me, you'd rather put your mind to dealing with a cash-flow problem than wading into the emotional muck, but it really is part of the job. There are significant costs but also benefits to going all in. The sooner you figure out what they are and how to deal with them, the better.

Chapter 7

Make Your Schedule Work for You

It's interesting how many people say things like, "Oh, it must be so great to be an entrepreneur—you control your own hours and you have so much freedom!" Usually, I simply nod and agree that, yes, it *is* great. Why burst their bubble? It's wonderful to daydream that maybe someday you too can set up your schedule in a way that allows you the freedom to go on field trips with your kids' class, knock off at 4 o'clock to play golf once a week, and take vacations during the shoulder season, when it's actually affordable. Frankly, that sounds appealing to me, too. But in reality, as you've no doubt gathered by now, it really is a dream. A pipe dream.

Theoretically, entrepreneurs do have the power to control their own schedules. And once you're well established, it might be possible to achieve a more flexible and personalized routine, provided you have enough support and are sufficiently self-disciplined. But until you've reached a particular level of success, you're almost certain to have much *less* control over your schedule than you would if you worked for someone else.

When you're first getting a business off the ground, you don't set your hours. Your customers do. If you don't have many of those yet, you will be spending every spare minute trying to drum some up. In the start-up phase, you'll be trying to network and create new connections whenever the opportunity arises. Often, it arises in the evening—at cocktail parties and other events perfectly scheduled to coincide with family dinners, your kids' school plays, and your friends' gatherings.

Expect really, really long hours, and plan that your work will regularly spill over into the weekend, too—and not just when you're first starting out. Once you're up and running, you won't be slowing down much. Even if you're in a position to hire, it will remain a one-person operation to a large extent. This is still your baby, and you'll likely have trouble handing it off to someone else even if the option to delegate exists. If you're not busy reviewing a balance sheet, updating your website, checking forecasts, hustling business, or figuring out what skill sets your next hire needs to have, don't worry. Before you know it, 10 more urgent tasks will pop up like ducks in a shooting gallery.

Remembering That There Is *Life After Business*

The rapid-fire, always-on schedule associated with launching a new venture or taking an existing business through a major growth phase will energize you—for a while. The charge you get from meeting tough challenges will invigorate you. During her first three years in business, Samantha Reynolds, the coffee-table book publisher, loved every minute. She worked all the time and, in her words, "didn't turn off at all." But then she woke up one day, spontaneously combusted, and said to herself, *I don't think I can do this tomorrow*. She realized she needed to stop working in her home, a renovated farmhouse, and find a separate work space; she also needed backup to help with the heavy lifting. So she moved her business to the top floor of a heritage building in Vancouver, where she built a custom bindery, and hired a full-time graphic designer. She no longer had to spend endless hours in the car, driving from graphic designer to printer. She'd created a stronger foundation for expansion, while achieving her initial goal of creating some breathing room for herself.

But not until her eighth year in business, when she could hire a full-time creative director, was she truly able to exhale. She thinks of that year as the one when she began to reclaim meaningful leisure. "I reconnected with friends, started a book club. My hobbies had sort of gone dormant. I hadn't read a novel since I started the company—not a single novel," she confesses. She hadn't felt she was missing out, and she hadn't felt resentful. Precisely because she loved her work, she had, she says, "forgotten the joy to be found in other things, like dinner parties and conversations." She'd also forgotten how to give herself permission simply to observe and enjoy calmly, rather than constantly producing and delivering. At first, she remembers, "It was awkward reoccupying a leisure space. It was like an atrophied muscle. I didn't really remember what people did when they weren't working."

She did make some changes and read some novels. But her schedule hasn't really changed all that radically over the years—she's taken only two vacations.

Even when you're calling the shots, you'll have to deal with the inherent unpredictability of an entrepreneur's schedule. You have to be flexible and you have to multi-task. In addition to your ongoing responsibilities as company skipper, you'll also be clapping a fireman's hat on your head and running around to put out fires regularly. These never occur at convenient moments, in my experience, and there's rarely any warning. Usually you have to shift focus on a moment's notice. The time you'll devote to managing crises will be taken, in large part, out of your family's hide. One of the reasons Kelsey Ramsden, whose company, Belvedere Place Development, handles large-scale construction projects, loves the entrepreneurial life is that she can take her kids (she has three under age seven) to doctors' appointments or accompany her eldest daughter, Sophie, on field trips at a moment's notice. But that flexibility works both ways. "If an emergency comes up and I'm the only guy who can deal with it, even if I'd already planned something with my daughter, it's like, 'Sorry, Soph, this has got to happen.'"

At first, I thought all I had to do was grow Venture, generate revenue, then hire great people. Surely after that I could hand off some of the most time-consuming tasks? But it doesn't work that way. The reality is that just when you think you have it all figured out, there will be another surprise—one that only you can handle—waiting just around the corner. If there isn't, you will create one for yourself—by deciding to expand, or retrench, or branch out into another area. So while on paper you have all the freedom in the world to control your own schedule, in real life, you're often a slave to it.

When I first became CEO at Venture, I was working close to 100 hours a week. I didn't run my schedule. It ran me. Sleep? Way down my list of priorities. Sometimes I went weeks without more than a few hours a night. I woke up at 3 a.m. regularly. Sometimes it was because I was having a full-blown panic attack, but other times I would jump out of bed because I'd had a brainstorm and wanted to make notes while it was still fresh in my mind.

Once the workday began, I hurled myself into it with abandon. That's when the fun really started. As CEO, I was supposed to be in charge, but no one had given me a manual on how to do my job. And aside from having once been the mother of four children under the age of seven—which equips you with some skills in crowd control, at least—I had zero training for it. Looking back, I'm reasonably certain that even if I'd had a formal business education, it wouldn't have helped that much. Textbook cases are one thing, on-the-ground realities quite another. It's not that I didn't expect long hours or that my adrenaline would be pumping overtime. I just didn't have any idea, really, that the pressure would never let up or that I'd have to switch hats, midstream, so frequently. One minute your HR person is knocking on your door; the next, your lawyer's on the phone. Then your accountant is clamouring for your attention. Meanwhile, your sales team is in the next room waiting for you to rally the troops. Every single day, you're dealing not only with a frenetic pace but also the feeling that everyone is counting on you to make the right calls. And that's because they are.

You can feel you're doing pretty well managing all this, and then, like clockwork, you're blindsided. I vividly remember, while I was trying to grow Venture, a conversation with my accountant that absolutely floored me. He said, "Look, you're in trouble. You need more cash." At first I laughed. I said, "What do you mean? We're adding new clients and growing the business!" He said, "Yes, but you're not figuring out how to make money at it. You're just growing resources. You're not taking the time to look at whether you're actually building a company that's profitable. There's growth, and then there's *profitable* growth."

I was stunned by that distinction. It just made no sense to me that the company was pulling in millions of dollars of revenue, and yet that wasn't enough. The accountant impressed on me that I'd better figure out how to solve my problem pretty quickly. But to do that, I needed to carve out time and mental space to mull things over. Picture yourself trying to find an opportunity to do either when you're working 100 hours a week.

Days hurtled by in a blur. And they never quite ended. You might be wondering how I managed housework. Well, often I didn't. I lived in fear that someone would drop by the house and see the chaos.

But ultimately I'm not unhappy I made the choices I did. If I'd been striving for work/life balance, my floors might have been cleaner and my kids might have had friends over more often. But my company wouldn't be what it is today, my children wouldn't have grown into the amazingly resilient and capable people they are today, and I wouldn't have had the breathtaking, dizzying, incredibly challenging, and interesting ride I've had.

Tailoring a Schedule to Suit Your Personality

There aren't hard-and-fast rules for organizing your time as an entrepreneur. If there were, considering how we feel about rules we didn't make up ourselves, we'd probably rebel against them anyway. Since there's no right or wrong method, you can be creative about how you structure your time. The trick lies in creating a schedule that's compatible with your real-life needs rather than your lofty ideals, then finding your own rhythm within it.

If you've always had a structured 9 to 5 job and are accustomed to having tasks assigned to you, you may find the idea of inventing your schedule from scratch every day daunting.

Perhaps you're worried you'll simply fritter all that time away. If you don't love your work and you're not driven, that's a real fear. Some people are most comfortable with a methodically planned routine. Entrepreneurs in this camp tend to run their lives like a military campaign. They're the ones who take scheduled breaks for exercise, eat meals at set times, and get dressed for the office even when they're spending the day hunched over a laptop at their kitchen table.

Other people find that a flexible schedule allows them to be more, not less, productive. Tony Lacavera, for instance, says he just can't accomplish nearly as much when his schedule is rigidly locked down. He much prefers to keep it as loose as possible. I feel the same way, much to the exasperation of the people who work with me. When there's room for spontaneity, there's also room to take advantage of unexpected opportunities—a longer conversation in the hallway when someone buttonholes you with a new idea, for instance.

Personally, I'm less a strict planner than a random doer. It's not that I don't have goals or a vision for my company or for myself. I do. But I zig and zag and operate much more in the moment, and this arrangement really works for me. I don't berate myself if I don't stay exactly on course, and I won't refuse to do something just because it doesn't seem to be directly related to achieving my goals. I love those spontaneous dinners, for instance, where I get to meet someone new and, instead of watching the clock, feel free to listen and really understand what drives that person and how she thinks. It's how I get some of my best ideas and how I've managed to build the emotional connections that have powered my company forward.

Whatever your approach, just be sure to structure your time

around an organizing principle that makes sense for your particular personality and your company's needs, then fill in from there. Maybe you'll get some ideas from seeing how four quite different entrepreneurs at different stages of life and different stages in the business cycle manage their time.

The Meticulous Planner

Annette Verschuren has had a remarkable career, much of it spent in the corporate sector, mostly in male-dominated industries. Annette grew up on a dairy farm in Cape Breton, but when she was 11, her dad had a major heart attack and was no longer up to the hard physical labour of running the farm. So Annette and her siblings took over. It was a crash course in crisis management, and she came out of it with a work ethic that you wouldn't believe. This is all the more notable because she has a hereditary kidney disorder and, between the ages of 15 and 21, had four operations to address it. When she was 16, Annette was so sick that she missed six months of school and, she says, "wanted to die." Pulling through that turned out to be life-defining. She emerged determined to make the most of every minute she had left.

At 20, fresh out of university, she got a job in the coal-mining sector—not, traditionally, a great place for women. From there, she went on to become executive vice-president of the Canada Development Investment Corporation and vice-president of corporate development for Imasco Ltd., where she gained experience in the tobacco industry. But what she really longed to do was to grow a company, and she realized she could land a leadership role faster in the retail sector. In 1993, when Annette was 37 years old, she became president and co-owner of the arts and crafts chain

Michaels Canada. After bringing the US company north of the border, she opened 17 stores in 26 months.

Earlier I told you about Bernie Marcus and Arthur Blank, the two guys who founded Home Depot after being given the boot by another hardware company. Well, when Annette was working at Michaels, a headhunter approached her: Home Depot's management team in Atlanta was looking for someone to help the Canadian branch of the company, which was struggling, and grow the business substantially. Talk about an opportunity! But when Annette learned that the Canadian CEO would have to work with the existing president in Atlanta, she said she wasn't interested. She didn't want to oversee a branch plant and answer to head honchos in another country. What she loved was running her own show, as she was doing at Michaels. "They were flabbergasted," she remembers. "I don't think anybody had ever said no to Home Depot."

And they respected her for being the first. Home Depot came back with what she calls "the deal of a lifetime," and in 1996 she became president and CEO of Home Depot Canada Inc. As promised, she was given free rein. Very few organizations would have given her the amount of autonomy she demanded, but she had two born entrepreneurs, Marcus and Blank, backing her. Annette felt protected because, she says, "they loved my entrepreneurialism."

Within two years, she had managed to increase cash flow to the point where it supported the Canadian company's growth. She took Home Depot Canada Inc. from 19 stores and $600 million in revenue in 1996 to 180 stores and $6 billion in revenue by 2011, when she left the company.

Why leave when you're doing such a great job? Annette just feels happier building a new enterprise than running a mature one. She took some time off to figure out her next act, and then, in October 2011, she and a partner started NRStor Inc., which develops technologies for storing renewable energy. How do you capture the energy created by the wind and the sun, and save it for later use? That's the question the Toronto-based company aims to answer.

"I don't go where it's easy," Annette, NRStor Inc.'s executive chairwoman, told *The Globe and Mail* in 2012, with typical understatement. "I was in home improvement; I was in coal mining and the tobacco business, so I've been in industries that are not for the weak-kneed. I'm 55 and I still have that one big one left in me."

Throughout much of her career, Annette has focused on building and expanding businesses owned, at least partially, by others. But operating within someone else's corporate structure has never stopped her from behaving like an entrepreneur or calling herself one. Not surprisingly for a farm girl who learned the value of discipline and organization as early as she did, she's a hard-core planner. She charts her schedule 18 months out, slotting in time for every aspect of her existence, even shopping. She says it's the only way she feels in control.

These days she gets up at 6 a.m., exercises for an hour, and then showers, eats breakfast, and leaves for her office in downtown Toronto. She has two or three meetings a day, and in between works with team members; when she has a board meeting, she blocks off serious chunks of time to read materials and prepare. At 6:30 or 7 p.m., she heads home to have dinner with her husband, Stan Shibinsky, who's retired and loves to cook.

It's really important to mention that virtually all the successful entrepreneurs I know are either addicted to fitness or include regular workouts in their schedules. Eight years ago, Annette decided to make her health as important a priority as her business. Aside from the obvious benefits, such as boosting her energy level and also boosting her confidence when she enters a room to do a presentation, she's convinced that her decision to set aside time in her schedule for regular exercise has lengthened her business career. She mentioned a study of male and female CFOs in which 77 percent of the male CFOs regularly got medical check-ups, but only 37 percent of the women did. In her view, there's a strong correlation between health and performance in stressful, high-level jobs, but women tend to be nurturers who focus on the needs of others instead of taking care of themselves. Annette made a conscious decision not to fall into that trap. She works out with a personal trainer every Tuesday, Thursday, and Saturday. "That's just the way it is," she says. "If I don't schedule it, if I don't have that discipline, I will miss it."

Annette doesn't travel as frequently for work as she once did, and she spends more time with Stan, whom she married in 2011, than she did with her first husband or the men she dated during the decade she was single after her divorce. Ever the planner, she books well ahead for special occasions, like going with Stan to Hawaii for a week to celebrate his birthday. She's well organized enough to do things like figure out how to take off for the month of August to hang out with her husband in Cape Breton. She manages that by working in the mornings, but afternoons and weekends are for golf and relaxation. She doesn't feel like a hamster on a wheel, forever running. In fact, she says she's never been happier.

The Random Doer

Remember serial inventor Wayne Fromm, the guy who cold-called Disney? He takes a much less regimented approach to his schedule, and goes wherever his passions—business or otherwise—lead him. He keeps "crazy hours" and sometimes gets so absorbed in his work that he loses track of time, then realizes he's been up for 48 hours—and hasn't eaten anything. His business takes him all over the world, but he's the opposite of world weary. Once, somebody asked him to meet up in Tokyo and he went for a day. His attitude is, Why not?

His enthusiasm about life is boundless. Wherever he is, he wakes up and begins checking out what's happening in other time zones. But he's equally excited to be at home in Toronto, where he regularly attends hot yoga classes with his daughter Sage, who's now in her mid-20s. He also plays tennis and squash, and hosts salon-type get-togethers for people from all walks of life. He puts a premium on spontaneity, and acknowledges that dating a doctor or lawyer probably wouldn't work, given his lifestyle. He's drawn to women who are available to pack up on impulse and go hiking in Peru.

Because Wayne's schedule is so free-floating, no two days are ever the same. He, too, is interested in health and wellness, so he might divert from a work task one afternoon to catch up on some *Dr. Oz* shows he's PVR'd. He also likes to micro-nap and boasts he can do it anywhere. Like many entrepreneurs, he's not a fan of meetings, so when he's forced to attend one, he gets there via rollerblades, figuring he might as well squeeze in some exercise en route. He doesn't like to waste time. (You can always spot the frustrated entrepreneurs in corporate meetings: they're the bored, fidgety ones who keep eyeing the exits.) One of the only standing meetings Wayne keeps is on Tuesday nights when he's in Toronto: dinner with his buddy of 20 years. That's one meeting he's always happy to go to.

His approach to the entrepreneurial lifestyle is to keep it fun and keep it unconventional. Doing things his way means not being bound by structures and customs he doesn't like or find helpful. However, he's quick to point out that he doesn't like chaos. He's not randomly zipping all over the place with no particular goal or purpose. In fact, he insists, "I'm very organized in my own way." His way works for him.

The Parent Entrepreneur

Dave Buckle, of Funk-Off fame, got his start in business when he was 22. At the time, he, his then girlfriend (now wife), Sarah, and a childhood friend embarked on their first venture: running a restaurant. Their partner's dad, an accountant, had a client who was looking to sell a diner. Although the restaurant business is notoriously risky and Dave's experience consisted mainly of delivering pizzas, "somehow," he says, they got a line of credit from the bank. (Having watched Dave pitch, I think the "somehow" is probably related to his blend of contagious enthusiasm and self-belief.) Sarah ran the front of the house, while Dave ran the kitchen. The business eventually dissolved, but they made decent money for a while and gained invaluable experience.

Today, besides running a body jewellery business together, Sarah and Dave also partner in a seasonal calendar business. They operate both businesses out of kiosks in malls. But that's not all: they also have an owner/operator contract with Hickory Farms, a company that sells premium meats and cheeses seasonally in large shopping malls.

Although the couple has had periods when they've pulled in a substantial income, Dave makes it clear that the desire to make a ton of money is not the driving force behind their life choices. Their interest is in "the journey, the experience." Right now, their priority is spending as much time as possible with their sons, who are eight and six. To that end, they're extremely deliberate about how they structure their time. "We build our lives with intention," Dave explains. "We don't have a lot of waking hours with our kids, so our focus is being at home with them when they're there."

They typically work evenings and weekends, but manage to spend a lot more time with their children than the lawyers, engineers, and corporate executives they know because they schedule their hours differently. That flexibility, says Dave, "is the most important thing in our lives." It's why they're entrepreneurs. "Being able to pick up the kids at 3:30 is the reason I do this. I will pass on a business opportunity if I can't pick them up after school. People who deal with me know that about me," he explains.

Dave and Sarah's day begins at 6:30 a.m., when their youngest son crawls into bed with them, followed shortly thereafter by the eight-year-old, and everyone snuggles until 7:15, when the morning routine kicks off. Dave drives the kids to school for 9 and picks them up at 3:30. "I enjoy being the last face they see in the morning and the first one they see at the end of their day," he says.

While the kids are at school, he and Sarah are taking care of business. After school, until the kids' weeknight bedtime around 7 or 7:30 p.m., the couple focuses on being parents. Usually they squeeze in another couple of hours of work every evening and on Saturdays. Many nights, they wind up working quite late; they deal with two manufacturing companies in Asia, and those emails don't start arriving until after the kids are in bed. During the Christmas season, when the malls stay open late seven days a week, they're up really late working the phones and burning the midnight oil overseeing their businesses.

When an emergency occurs, which Dave says happens approximately all the time, "You have to deal with it. If somebody calls in sick and I have to go in and I have the kids with me, guess what? They're coming along. They love it, so I don't get a fight. Sure, it's challenging in a retail environment with little ones running around. But my attitude is, 'Hey, I'm a business owner and my kids are here.' Anyone rational will get that. And if they don't, frankly I don't care."

The "Retiree"

In Chapter 5 you met Yung Wu, who spent eight years learning the ropes in the corporate world before launching his business software company in 1990. During the start-up phase, Yung put in 20 hours a day, seven days a week. But work didn't exactly slow to a crawl after that: the company grew at a rate of 70 to 80 percent annually for the first five years, and by 1995 it employed about 100 people. Yet Yung and his co-founder continued to do all the partnership-building, interviewing, hiring, organizing, proposal development, sales, and travelling. In other words, five years in, Yung was still logging 15 to 18 hours a day, seven days a week.

Today, as managing director of the venture accelerator NFQ Ventures (which stands for "Never Fu@#ing Quit"), he plays more of an overseer role and likes to joke that now he's retired. In case you're wondering what "slowing down" means in entrepreneur-speak, Yung graciously took notes one day to track how he spent his time. Here's what his day looked like:

5:48 a.m.—wake up

5:53 a.m.—check in w/body telemetry (BP, RHR, sleep pattern monitor, weight, body mass index)

5:58 a.m.—give dog morning treats

6:03 a.m.—daily supplements (2000 mg Vit C, Vit B/B+) + light breakfast + iPAD reading

6:10 a.m.—browse feeds from Twitter, Bloomberg, *The Economist*, email (+ Raptors news)

7:00 a.m.—best. coffee. ever. (Lavazza Rossa espresso w/Jura coffee machine)!

7:05 a.m.—scan Fuse analytics dashboard to check movement on installs, revenue, ARPDAU, rank

7:20 a.m.—preview headlines

7:30 a.m.—scan calendar for day's schedule

7:40 a.m.—answer own questions: What did I learn yesterday? What's the outlook for the next 60–90 days? What are the priorities for the day & week? What is the major impact & outcome I want to achieve today? Who should I work with to orchestrate that outcome?

8:11 a.m.—shower & get set for day

8:28 a.m.—walk to work (taking the long route)

9:03 a.m.—check in w/NFQ partners on portfolio & investee deal flow

9:30 a.m.—check in w/Fuse senior team

9:45 a.m.—build & publish agenda for weekly senior leadership team of investee company meeting in afternoon

10:00 a.m.—call with founder & CEO of investee company to compare notes on direction, strategy, team goals

10:30 a.m.—coach founder & work with him to sort out major priorities & especially to refine & synthesize strategy/plan, &

sort out timing, resourcing & sequencing of next steps

11:02 a.m.—check on email threads, mobile analytics dashboard

11:16 a.m.—work with Bus Dev executive on major accounts outlook, qualified deal flow, & resourcing & staffing decisions to get more balance in complement of "hunters" vs. "farmers" in the sales team

12:30 p.m.—lunch break, check on Bloomberg, buy & sell stocks

1:30 p.m.—senior leadership team weekly meeting: check in by each member of the team; forecasts on customer, shareholder, & employee goals; discuss employee performance (in terms of skill, will, & fit) for one of the business units, etc.; review key decisions & adjusted priorities

3:30 p.m.—worst. coffee. ever (cafeteria blend)

3:36 p.m.—review external board agenda & materials

4:00 p.m.—walk to board meeting (taking the short route)

6:37 p.m.—get back home

6:45 p.m.—raid the refrigerator & the pantry

7:30 p.m.—dinner with Katrina, talk to my parents

9:30 p.m.—ponder some interesting questions that arose in discussion with colleague

10:00 p.m.—evening news

11:00 p.m.—browse Twitter, email, Facebook, Google I, LinkedIn

12:05 a.m.—reflect on day, & remind self of how lucky I am to be in situation that I'm in, & how fortunate to have my friends & family

12:45 a.m.—read chapters on Kindle for iPad from *Oryx and Crake* by Margaret Atwood & *Venture Deals* by Brad Feld & Jason Mendelson

1:34 a.m.—pack it in for the day

Yung acknowledges that his hours are still nuts, but what's different these days is that his time belongs to him much more than when he was actively running his own business. "Then need drove where I spent my time. I would take any meeting and participate in every sales call. Now I get to make choices." These days they include attending fewer cocktail parties and events, and spending more time with his wife Katrina and his family and friends.

* * *

So there you have it—what four different versions of independence look like under a microscope. Your version will look different, of course. It will be dictated by the type of person you are, what stage of life you're at, whether you have a family or not, and what your business is. But one thing is clear: the demands and pace do not miraculously slacken once you've achieved some success. Annette, Wayne, Dave, and Yung have all done that, and they are all still working long hours. Yet, all four of them love their lives. They don't resent the hours they keep and they don't complain of feeling burned out.

Another thing that won't lessen with success? The need for your leadership. Your ability to develop the inner reserves you need to inspire people, create change, and navigate the occasional emotional minefields—in other words, your ability to lead—will become more and more important as you, and your business, grow and mature.

Let's take a look at what's in store.

Chapter 8

Learning to Lead

The paradox of independence and go-it-alone emotional resilience is that they exert a magnetic pull on others. The more you put yourself out there, talk about your vision, and grow your business, the more people you'll attract, whether they be employees, clients, partners, or investors. And this phenomenon opens the door to a whole new challenge: leadership. While entrepreneurs are born with a host of unique skills and talents, the ability to lead is not necessarily one of them. This gap can be a huge challenge as your business grows and the nature of your job as founder changes.

When I bought out my last partner and later went from being president to CEO at Venture, it took me a long time to find my footing. You'd think I'd have been happy to take command, but initially I felt quite lost and lonely. I no longer had a lineup of people at my door looking to me to solve their problems. The president had a more hands-on role in day-to-day operations, and I not only missed the action but wasn't truly certain how to frame the role I now had. Where should I spend my time? How should

I interact with the team without stepping on the president's toes? Now my job was to keep the company on course, streamline the organization, and take hurdles out of people's way. Consequently, a great deal of my time involved planning strategy and talking to legal and financial advisers. My contribution seemed much less tangible. I felt like a star athlete who'd suddenly been benched.

I also somewhat missed having partners. I hadn't realized how much I'd relied on their knowledge. I was used to bouncing ideas off them and seeking their input. And support. Now it was all down to me, and the learning curve was steep. For all the times I had cursed having partners, I started to better understand how many twirling plates were in the air that they had helped manage. I'd worked my way into the highest leadership position in the company, yet didn't *really* understand a balance sheet! I mean, I knew what a balance sheet was, of course, but I didn't truly grasp the implications of all the numbers. It took my CFO sitting me down and saying, "We have to talk."

There was another significant challenge: delegating. This didn't come easily to me after years of being in the trenches and knowing what was happening on the front lines. I could see it with my own eyes. When you're the general, you have to depend heavily on the information your lieutenants provide. Unless you trust them implicitly, you're always looking over their shoulders and second-guessing their decisions. Even if you do trust them, you still may be doing that because you just don't want to let go. Of anything.

Relinquishing control is torture for entrepreneurs. If you want to know what it feels like, picture a two-year-old with his favourite blanket. Now, make blankie go bye-bye. Cut to major freak-out. Like the average stubborn toddler, entrepreneurs want to have their own way. And when someone decides otherwise, we stamp our feet and shout, "No!"

This reaction can kill a company, though. Some entrepreneurs simply will not listen to customers, lenders, or employees. They won't part with equity; they'd rather over-borrow and are therefore extremely vulnerable if there's an economic downturn. A 2011 Ernst & Young report talks about the "narcissism trap"—when the fervent self-belief that propels an entrepreneur to success outlasts its use and becomes a blinder. Leaders who dismiss anyone who questions their vision as "negative" or "not a team player" may even subconsciously *want* their company to fail. If they go bankrupt, they no longer have to deal with their intense anxiety about failure and can start over. By refusing to delegate, many become their own worst enemies.

When an entrepreneur moves into a managerial role, she has to trust the people she's hired and create a climate where they feel free to challenge both her and the status quo. Part of creating that environment is being sure that you listen carefully to what they're saying, and if you disagree, do so without being dismissive. But entrepreneurs tend to be impatient by nature. We're inclined to interrupt, barrel ahead, and steamroll right over those in our path. If you're at all like me, you'll have to work hard to keep your worst impulses in check.

This is where it's really helpful to check in with the one thing that launched the whole show in the first place: your vision. Many entrepreneurs—me included—feel most comfortable when we're the ones calling the shots. But failing to listen to other people is a surefire way to stymie your growth—and your ability to reach your vision—because you simply can't have all the answers all the time. "You've got to be resolute in your view that you have an idea worth pursuing," says seafood magnate John Risley. "But you've got to listen to people who can help you implement the plan to get value out of that idea." It gets back to the old hiring adage about surrounding yourself with people who are smarter than you. You can fill your team with enough brain cells to light up a city, but if you're not willing to listen, it's a waste of time and money.

Yet you also have to communicate that certain decisions are non-negotiable. Decisions that threaten to compromise your company's values or your own vision will not be implemented. Period. It can be extremely difficult to protect your vision once your company has grown a bit, and if you shy away from conflict and live to make others happy, you're toast. People will try to chip away at your vision all the time, often by telling you that what you're seeking to do is impossible. But there's a fine line between sticking to your vision and being a slave-driver—or being perceived as so in charge that no one dares question you. When I took the reins at Venture, I realized I had to be completely clear about when I was merely expressing my opinion and when I was issuing a directive. I remember a meeting where I held forth about some marketing materials. I had to leave early, but I assumed we'd have further discussions and intended to give the matter more thought. My staff, however, took what I'd said as a de facto request and executed the materials. What I learned from that experience was that while I didn't see myself any differently now that I was CEO, others did. As the leader of the company, my views were perceived to carry a lot more weight. When I expressed an opinion, I had to keep that in mind.

It took me a few years and some big mistakes before I'd defined my new role as a leader and fully embraced it. That experience is fairly common for entrepreneurs. When Diana Olsen owned one

Balzac's café, she knew all her customers by name and could also tell you their drinks of choice. Now that she's running eight cafés, she can't even tell you the names of half the baristas she employs. For a while, she felt very bad about losing that close connection with her staff and customers. Then she just realized "that's the way it is."

When a fire forced Samantha Reynolds to relocate her publishing company in 2012, she sheepishly confessed that it was, in a weird way, a little thrilling: starting over felt a bit like a start-up. She felt guilty even saying it, though. No one had been hurt in the fire, and the company's data was all off-site, so none of the clients' irreplaceable memorabilia had been damaged. But she was still horrified that she could even *think* about getting a buzz out of something essentially destructive. Plus, the fire had caused so many headaches and so much extra work for her staff. And yet . . . She had to admit that it felt good, being forced to call on her crisis-management skills under pressure, just as she'd had to in the early days. It rekindled something inside that she hadn't even been aware she'd missed.

When your company is well established, it's a wonderful feeling. You've made it! And on some days, your heart will burst with pride watching the company you've created blossom before your eyes. But you will still have days that scare you, break your heart, and leave you feeling incredibly lonely. In a way, that's good news: there will always be new challenges and new things to learn and master.

Advice: Learning When to Take It

When it comes to leadership, you always have to balance your need to trust yourself and the value of outside advice. Getting the right advice and being willing to act on it can transform an entre-preneur's fortunes. But sometimes advice is hard to hear, because it feels like or is, in fact, a criticism of you or your way of doing things. Sometimes, however, it's the only way to grow.

Singer-songwriter Jann Arden—who has 17 top ten singles and eight Juno awards—also knows that sometimes you need a push to get to the next level. Seven or eight years ago, she was experiencing terrible stage fright and had convinced herself that her performing days were over. She considered going back to school. She told CBC Radio's Jian Ghomeshi that she was think-ing of farming pigs and growing pot in Springbank, Alberta. Then music manager Bruce Allen called, saying he wanted to work with her. (His client list includes Michael Bublé and Anne Murray, among other leading lights.) He didn't baby her or psychoanalyze her when she told him about the stage fright. Instead, he assessed the situation and gave her a kick in the butt. He told her: "You've got so much left to do. Just go out there and goddam do it."

Jann found Allen's directness both comforting and famil-iar: he was just like her dad. She values his honesty: Allen won't hesitate to tell her straight out if her outfit doesn't look good. She's flourished under his guidance and believes the memoir and album she subsequently wrote and released might not exist if he hadn't come into her life.

Samantha Reynolds also welcomed the input of a mentor: the husband of a woman who'd commissioned a tribute book in his honour as a surprise. He was so moved and impressed by the book Samantha created that he wanted to meet her. "He saw a good idea for a company being run by a young, naive woman, and I think he just couldn't help himself. He really believed in what I was doing, but he saw that I wasn't doing it sustainably. He thought, *If she'll listen to me, I can help her.*"

Looking back, Samantha says the guy "just good-naturedly bullied" her into agreeing to be mentored, then gave her some stern advice: if she wanted to build a sustainable company, she had to pay her employees more and go after a different type of client. The salaries she'd been paying employees were fine for a bunch of 20-year-olds, but eventually, her mentor pointed out, they'd want to have kids and buy homes. He made her see that if she wanted to keep her team and attract more good people, she'd have to pay a respectable wage—and to do that, she'd have to charge more for her services, and that meant going after work that commanded a higher price. Accordingly, in 2005, Echo Memoirs shifted its focus from wedding books, pet books, and the like, to the two core areas the company concentrates on today: corporate memoirs and personal biographies.

Since then, Samantha has had other influential mentors who come in "completely different personality shapes." But none of them are cheerleaders, nor would she want them to be. "I have lots of people in my life who support and believe in me. I look for people I respect who really provoke me and unsettle me."

Advice: Taking It with a Grain of Salt or Embracing It with Open Arms

One day an angel may land on your shoulder and whisper such wise counsel in your ear that you'd be crazy not to take it. But not all advice will be so good, and if you fall into the trap of leaning too heavily on advisers, you run the risk of abdicating your leadership role and letting others run your show.

When I first started out, I was so in awe of CFOs, accountants, and lawyers that I tended to take their word as gospel. After all, who was I to question their advice? I had a high school education and they were highly trained professionals. But one day a friend told me about some challenges he'd faced selling his company. Finally, he said, "I told the lawyers and accountants to get out of the way."

I was shocked. "Are you telling me you didn't take their advice?" I asked. "Isn't that what you're paying them for?"

He had a different take altogether. His view was that it's the job of CFOs, lawyers, and accountants to bring the entrepreneur up to speed on all the risks and everything that could go wrong, and the entrepreneur's responsibility to listen and become fully informed about potential hazards. But at the end of the day, the entrepreneur has to put everything in perspective and make the final decision about how to push through the roadblocks, achieve the goal, and then instruct his advisers to execute his decision. If you can't do this, too, you'll never get there.

For the first time, I understood the difference between somebody whose job it is to keep me well informed and somebody whose job it is to make decisions and reach conclusions. Once I understood that a professional's job was not to talk me out of what I wanted to achieve, but rather to advise me, protect me, and help me structure things in a way designed to help me achieve my desired result, I started to have very different conversations with my advisers.

Once you've made a decision and figured out *what* you're going to do, professional advisers can be invaluable in helping you figure out *how* to make your goals happen. After years of relying on his own "trial and error" approach to growth, Calgary entrepreneur Derek Bullen discovered how to get the most out of professional advisers—a move that would help his IT staffing business, S.i. Systems, achieve atmospheric growth.

It was 1999, and Derek had built up his firm to roughly $5 million in annual sales when he invited a seasoned entrepreneur to buy a 15 percent stake in the company. Derek's hope was that his new partner and mentor would help him grow the company more than he could on his own. Over time, the pair decided that they wanted the company to grow from roughly $5 million to $100 million in sales. Derek immediately started mulling over *how* he was going to create such high-octane growth when his partner urged him to make the biggest single layout of cash he'd made since he started his business.

"He told me to go out and hire a company that makes business plans for companies that do $100 million a year in sales," Derek remembers. The price tag? A hundred grand. Over the next few months, the consultants studied Derek's company, the marketplace, and the economy, then put together an in-depth business plan designed to help him achieve massive growth in a five- to 10-year period. Most of what the firm suggested, Derek says, he would never have thought of on his own. For example, the company suggested S.i. Systems raise $2 million for a proprietary enterprise software system. The consultants also suggested a number of strategic acquisitions of IT staffing agencies in other parts of the country.

On the one hand, Derek was thrilled with the overall plan. On the other, he felt uncomfortable with the degree of change. "It was very different from anything I'd ever done before," Derek explains. And he was worried about "losing control" over daily decisions. What's more, Derek would be bearing the risk of implementing any of the strategies laid out in the plan—strategies that, for the first time ever, he hadn't devised mostly on his own. "It was scary. I was still focused on short-term growth, but this plan was built for the long term." Derek credits his mentor and partner for getting him through. "He was more experienced and was more comfortable looking that far into the future than I was." When Derek started doubting himself or the plan, he'd check in with his partner, who coached him through his fears. In 2006, S.i. Systems hit roughly $50 million in sales, and that number doubled the following year. In 2013, the company is slated to bring in close to $300 million in revenue—all of it from the $100,000 business plan.

Learning to Lower the Boom

One of the toughest things you have to do as a leader is to let people on your team go. This is hard even though, for many entrepreneurs, getting fired is a rite of passage and something of a badge of honour. A lot of us brag about what bad employees we were. Here's a partial list of those who were given the heave-ho earlier on in their careers: Madonna, Marc Jacobs, Jerry Seinfeld, Oprah, Lee Iacocca, Michael Bloomberg—and my personal favourite, Elvis. Legend has it that after Elvis's first appearance at the Grand Ole Opry, the manager of the concert hall told him he'd be better off returning to his previous job as a truck driver.

In fact, many entrepreneurs and creative types say that getting fired wound up helping their careers. They figured out they were on the wrong career path, or it was character-building in all the right ways. Anna Wintour, Condé Nast artistic director and legendary editor-in-chief of *Vogue*, told attendees at a *Teen Vogue* Fashion University appearance that she got the axe after nine months as a junior fashion editor at *Harper's Bazaar* because the editor thought her cutting-edge fashion shoots were *too* edgy. Wintour, famously nicknamed "Nuclear Wintour" for her chilly and unemotional manner with employees, recommended to the fashion students that they all get fired at some point. She considered it to have been a great learning experience.

In his 2005 Stanford University commencement address, Steve Jobs also sang the praises of getting sacked. Shortly after he turned 30, by which time he'd built Apple into a $2 billon company with over 4,000 employees, he was kicked out of his own company. The ouster was highly public and felt highly personal. After a few months of beating himself up and considering running away from Silicon Valley, he began to realize that while he'd been rejected, he was still in love: with being an entrepreneur. So he decided to start over. In 1985, the same year he left Apple, he founded NeXT, a computer company that developed and manufactured computer workstations; the following year he acquired the computer graphics division of Lucasfilm, which became Pixar, where he served as CEO and majority shareholder until Disney bought the company in 2006. "The heaviness of being successful was replaced by the lightness of being a beginner again, less sure about everything," Jobs said in 2005. "It freed me to enter one of the most creative periods of my life."

So getting turfed can be a beautifully liberating and enriching experience. But having to turf someone is not. For me it was agonizing, and I still rank it one of my least favourite tasks. The first time I had to fire someone, it took me weeks to muster my courage. I'd known for months that the person was wrong for the company, but every time I thought about verbalizing that fact to the person's face, I felt sick to my stomach. I completely over-thought the situation. I even remember crying about it. I was a total mess. When the day came, somehow I got through it. And as soon as the deed was done, the person looked at me and said, "I'm really relieved. The job wasn't right for me, either."

I couldn't believe it. Here I'd agonized for months, lived in abject fear, felt horribly guilty that I was ruining someone's life, and for what? All that angst was totally unnecessary. It would have been wiser simply to rip the band-aid off and do us both a favour.

Today, I look at my relationships with employees as a business arrangement, not life-long emotional commitments. If it isn't working out, I end it, as quickly as possible. Doing it is never going to feel good, but I try to remind myself that in the end, this may turn out to be a lucky break for the person. She may be the next Steve Jobs and just not know it yet.

I'd be lying if I said the worst part about holding on to ill-suited employees is that you're holding *them* back from *their* dreams. The truth is, you could be holding your company back as well. Custom-label manufacturer Mabel's Labels is a great example. In 2003, when the company launched, the firm was headquartered in the basement of one of the founders. "We made decisions sitting on a couch in my sister's basement with a cup of tea," remembers Julie Cole, who founded the firm with her sister, sister-in-law, and best friend (who also happened to marry Julie's young uncle). The atmosphere was close knit, the founders were always accessible. But as the company has grown, so too have the demands on Julie and her partners. While some early employees embraced the growth, others resented it. "Some would tell us, 'We don't see you guys anymore; you're always in boardrooms.' You're going to have some employees who are excited about growth. And you're going to have some people who won't survive it. And you have to be okay with that," Julie says.

The Trouble with Partners

Maybe you're thinking you'd rather not lead a business alone. A partner could bring in some cash and offer you a shoulder to lean on in tough times. Having someone to share in the challenges and the triumphs of an entrepreneurial venture is tempting, but business partnerships are rarely simple.

Many entrepreneurs compare business partnerships to marriages, and with good reason. When they work, they're a thing of beauty; when they don't, they can wreak havoc in your life and your company's like nothing else. The best ones are collaborative and nourishing; the worst end bitterly, and can involve gut-wrenching fallout. Some former business partners won't acknowledge each other if they pass on the street. Others badmouth one another so vigorously that they sound worse than divorced exes. All of which is to say that before you get into bed with someone, business-wise, do your due diligence.

A lot of people think the most important skill you need as an entrepreneur is a head for business, but I'd argue that learning how to read people is equally if not more important. When I'm considering partnering with someone, I don't just look at balance sheets and bottom lines. I try to determine whether that person is a safe bet psychologically. You can glean a lot simply by observing their behaviour, so I try to pay close attention to what they do, not just what they say. Do they listen as much or more than they talk? Do they treat the person serving them coffee with kindness and respect? These simple actions can reveal a lot about someone's character.

Most importantly, you have to have some mechanism for handling conflict. No matter how beautifully you get along, you're going to disagree on occasion. If you feel that you can't, that any conflict feels too personal, you're in trouble. Jann Arden learned this lesson the hard way, after having to sever a few business relationships that were so personal, it felt like she was getting divorced. "You're like a close-knit family, but sometimes you come to a fork in the road," she says.

The breakup of her business partnership with her longtime promoter was particularly devastating. They formed a management company and worked closely together for a decade. Everything was perfect, until it wasn't. When they parted ways, things were far from amicable. The former friends wound up in litigation. Today, Jann says she wishes they'd been able to sit down and have a frank talk long before matters reached that point. But because they'd become so close, it felt impossible to Jann to act like a boss. The takeaway for her was that "you can't be a leader and run a company and be somebody's great friend. I never thought those words would come out of my mouth." These days, she's a stickler for respecting boundaries. "I've been very careful not to create a situation where I can't be the boss."

Just like the best marriages, the best business partnerships I've observed are based on trust, mutual respect, complementary skills, personalities, and a healthy willingness to work through and address differences. Funk-Off co-founders Dave Buckle and Trevor Fronchak were friends long before they became partners, and Dave considers their arrangement so idyllic personally and professionally that, he says, "If Trevor were a girl, I could have married him." Carbon Farmer's Brad Rabiey says of his wife Rebecca, "Together, we're a good entrepreneur." They're both optimists, but he's more the risk-taker whereas she's more careful about money. "I call her my Senate. She's my sober second thought," he says. Then there's Balzac's owner Diana Olsen, who feels so comfortable discussing problems with her staff that she almost considers them to be her business partners. In fact, two of them do own shares in the company. During tough times, when she needed their commitment but couldn't pay them what they deserved, she offered them the chance to earn equity over time. The arrangement has worked splendidly. From my view as her business partner, along with Bruce Croxon, she has shown herself to be a good communicator who reaches out when she knows she needs help.

I'd have to say that Chris Emery and Larry Finnson of OMG's Candy have one of the most yin-yang business partnerships I've ever observed. They finish each other's sentences just like a long-married couple. And in a way, I guess, you could also call them high school sweethearts: they've been buddies since then. But things weren't always so rosy. OMG is actually a remarriage of sorts for the pair, who parted ways after co-founding Krave's, the confectionary company they launched out of their Winnipeg basements in 1996. That partnership lasted 10 years, during which time they manufactured and marketed Clodhoppers—fudge and graham wafer clusters concocted from Chris's grandmother's recipe. The brand generated $9 million in sales and landed on the shelves of Zellers, Costco, Shoppers Drug Mart, and Wal-Mart. In 2006, Brookside Foods—a chocolate company now owned by Hershey's—bought the pair out.

Then their friendship went through a dark patch. Chris went to Brookside, while Larry pursued his other ventures. But over time, they realized they missed working together and sharing a passion. They spoke on and off after going their separate ways; then, in 2009, Larry started working with Brookside as well, to promote Clodhoppers. That's when they decided to partner up again after their non-compete agreements ended in 2011.

During their Clodhoppers days, both were in their 20s. They had such heated fights then that once Larry put his fist through the drywall. They now admit the conflicts were driven by insecurity. "They were about, Who's the man? Who's running the business? Who's coming up with the best decisions?" said Chris. "It almost became more about who could win the argument than what was best for the company."

Now both in their 40s, they say they've learned from their mistakes and joke that now they're probably just too old and exhausted to have knock-'em-down fights anymore. At Krave's, Larry was president and Chris vice-president. At OMG, they're co-presidents. Their skills do cross over in certain ways—Larry's lean more toward operations and finance, while Chris's favour sales and marketing—but they're both actively involved in running all business operations, and they both weigh in on all major decisions. And like many successfully married couples, when they're angry, they give themselves a day to cool off before attempting to work stuff out. To illustrate how far he's come, Larry told me he was so frustrated with his son's coach recently, that "10 years ago, I'd have ripped into him instantly. This time, I waited, talked to him calmly 24 hours later, and got my point across." Apparently he's such a changed man that even his mom gave him points for not blowing his top. As for managing his temper in his partnership with Chris: "There'll always be fireworks. You've got to have that passion and fire. But now it's about what's best for the company."

Since their appearance on *Dragons' Den*, I have become a partner in OMG Candy and I see first-hand how this successful collaboration works. We all have a role to play.

Really, Really, Really, Really Bad Days

I can't really wrap up a chapter on leadership if I don't spend some time talking about leading during heartbreaks and horrible days. The question is not whether you'll have days when all hell is breaking loose and you have to be the calm general, but how you'll handle them when you do.

Maybe you'll be checking out a trade show and discover that someone seems to have knocked off one of your many patented inventions. Wayne Fromm knows what that feels like. It knocks the wind right out of you. And then you feel like you're going to explode.

Maybe you'll have a lucrative contract with an international brand, spelling out how you're going to own and operate eight stores, and then suddenly there's a buyout, you're kicked to the curb, and a massive portion of your income evaporates overnight. Worse, you'll have to tell your general manager, who also happens to be your good friend—and a young single dad who's just signed a mortgage—that in a few days he's going to be out of work. That's a day that still haunts Dave Buckle.

Maybe you'll build a scrappy little company and play David to the Goliath of the country's Big Three mobile providers (who, by the way, once lobbied to block your launch—prompting the CRTC to shut you down for two months, while you tore through tens of millions of dollars), only to be bought out and face the prospect that your company could be sold to one of those Goliaths. Tony Lacavera has a good idea what that feels like.

When you have bad moments, your only choices are to succumb and give up or learn from them and carry on. Entrepreneurs simply aren't wired to do the former. Wayne Fromm said that when he sees someone has knocked off one of his patented ideas, he finds it more infuriating than anything else. "I go ballistic. I feel the same way you'd feel if someone had cheated on you in a relationship. But it comes with the territory. I bet whoever invented the wheel was knocked off as well. So I'm more weathered now. I've learned to control my emotions—otherwise, they'll poison you. I just make up my mind to be the best brand, the first to market, the one to make Oprah's List and to be featured on the *Today Show*." (He achieved those goals with Quik Pod, the first hand-held single-leg tripod for smartphone cameras, which was also featured on the *Tonight Show* with Jay Leno.)

Remember Yung Wu's emotional reckoning after 9/11? His software company had grown from two people to 400, and was worth about $200 million. But after 9/11 the financial services infrastructure collapsed, and Castek went from winning 60 to 70 percent of the deals in its sector to not having any customers to make a deal with for 18 months. By 2003, the company's business had dried up. The only option was to go from 400 people to 16.

Yung had been personally involved in hiring every single one of the company's employees. They were like family to him and to one other. In fact, many had met their spouses in the company and were now married with children. He remembers standing in the auditorium on the day he had to make the announcement and looking out at all the faces, knowing that nine out of 10 of the people staring fearfully back at him were going to lose their jobs. "It was the worst day of my life," he says simply.

Until that moment, he'd thought he was invincible. "We were two guys, then four, then 10, then 18. . . . We were constantly taking risks, beating companies a hundred times our size, winning jobs like Air Canada and Bank of Canada. I'd escaped every single death blow. I thought I was like that guy in the movies who's standing there with bullets coming at him while everybody else is hiding, and not a bullet scratches him."

Bloodied but determined, Yung and his team managed to build the company back up to 200 people before selling it to Oracle in 2007. If he'd thrown in the towel in 2003, as his team wanted him to do, Yung says, "I'd be the guy that blew hundreds of millions of dollars for shareholders on one of the most promising tech companies in Canada." But because he hung on, that wasn't his legacy. Survival, he says, isn't rocket science. "It wasn't that I was terribly brilliant. Some days you just have to get up in the morning and be willing to put your left shoe on and your right shoe on and keep on keeping on. And eventually things turn around."

* * *

Running a business is challenging, no doubt about it. As the business changes, so do the challenges. The pressures on you to lead will sometimes feel enormous. They never go away altogether. And some of the emotional aspects of the entrepreneurial lifestyle become more intense as your business is more established. You have more skin in the game, more ego invested, more time sunk in—and you have new responsibilities and are dealing with new expectations, too.

On the home front there are also going to be new emotional challenges. Let's look at those next.

Chapter 9

Balancing the Emotional Ledger at Home

Entrepreneurship can be hard on your home life. When you're all in, so are the people who love you, whether they want to be or not. It's really important to remember that the people you're closest to didn't choose independence—they had *yours* thrust on them. And there's something else: unless you're living alone, you're not independent at home. You're interdependent. You need your family's support and you care (or should care) about their needs, too.

This is the case for workers of all stripes. Most people I know—entrepreneurs or otherwise—teeter on the edge of work-aholism and have more commitments than they can handle. But the reality is that the families of entrepreneurs have to put up with a lot. In fact, the impact of your lifestyle is almost certain to be profound and far-ranging—a bit like an earthquake, really, only the aftershocks never really stop. And there's the potential for complete destruction: I don't know many entrepreneurs who haven't been through divorce or come perilously close.

When our family dynamics fail, it's very often because neither party had realistic expectations about the demands of the lifestyle. That's good news, in my opinion: it means that if you anticipate and prepare realistically, you stand a much better chance of disaster-proofing your most important personal relationships. Even so, it's unlikely you're going to cruise along without hitting any bumps in the road—particularly if you're living with someone who has a life and dreams of his or her own. But at least if you're alert to the dangers, you're more likely to be aware when you're stumbling into a relationship red zone, and that means you'll have a better chance of exiting. Together.

Living with an Entrepreneur

For the entrepreneur, life is work and work is life. For us, that's cause for celebration a lot of the time. For those around us, not so much. Our lack of boundaries between personal and professional life can be very hard on our families, who are inevitably drawn into and affected by our business choices. In essence, they're on the entrepreneurial roller coaster, too, whether they enjoy it or not. But unless they're prepared to bail on the relationship alto-gether, they also have to stay on, even if they're white-knuckling it, even if they're losing their lunch.

Often they also have skin in the game: the family home may be mortgaged to support the business, RRSPs may have been cashed, almost certainly the family risked at least one income. And then there are our expectations: that they'll believe in us unreservedly, listen patiently while we drone on about the company ad nau-seam, and cheerfully accept the fact that we can't always be there for them when they need us and may never be able to split the domestic responsibilities 50/50.

It's a lot to ask.

The highs and lows of sharing a home with an entrepreneur don't just come from the business, either. Entrepreneurs themselves usually aren't the steadiest and calmest of characters. Cameron Herold, former chief operating officer of 1-800-Got-Junk, founded and runs Vancouver-based BackPocket COO, which coaches businesses and mentors CEOs. As reported on CBS News, at a presentation to 300 CEOs, Herold read out a list of traits shared by successful entrepreneurs and asked audience members to stand up after they'd heard five that they believed they possessed. By the time he'd listed nine—including "flooded with ideas," "driven," "restless and unable to keep still," "easily irritated by minor obstacles"—95 percent of the entrepreneurs were on their feet. That's when he told them he was actually reading from a list used to diagnose bipolar disorder.

Herold wasn't suggesting that all entrepreneurs need therapeutic help (although I suppose a compelling case could be made for that, too). He was simply pointing out that many of us have manic-depressive tendencies. What really resonated with me was his comment that when entrepreneurs are on a high, they tend to share their excitement with other entrepreneurs; but when their moods head south (when they're consumed with self-doubt, say, or stressed beyond the max), they don't usually let on to other entrepreneurs that they're feeling low.

However, stoic as entrepreneurs can be, we're not known for suffering in silence. Herold didn't say it, but I think we all know who entrepreneurs lean on when they're feeling low: our significant others (if they haven't already fled, that is). Nor did he say this, but I will: when we're careening between exhilaration and despair, we're hell to live with.

Even when we're not careening between two polar emotions, we're often *still* not present—we're in entrepreneurial la-la land, figuring out some problem or thinking over some new strategy. And while many people in today's overworked society may share this experience for months or even years of their careers, for entrepreneurs this always-on mentality lasts, well, *forever*. We never really close the door on our work, which can be very tough on our families, especially our spouses. Picture this: you arrive home from work at 9 p.m. and your long-suffering partner says, "You're finally home." Unless he's also an entrepreneur, he's been waiting to spend time with you. Probably not sitting around twiddling his thumbs with nothing better to do than watch the door and pray you'll walk through it, but waiting nonetheless. But when you do walk in the door, you're distracted. Let's say you had a run-in with one of your employees that day, and the incident is on your mind. It bothered you so much that you can't just let go of it when you cross the threshold. In fact, you'd like to vent for 30 or 40 minutes and get some help figuring out what to do. However, the look on your spouse's face when you mention this is not encouraging. Maybe he even grumbles, "Here we go again." He's sick of hearing you talk business. Are you ever again going to have a conversation about anything else? Like, say, *his* day? I think you can probably write the rest of this scene.

Or let's say you waltz through the door, bubbling with excitement. You've landed an important client, you're on cloud nine, and you want your spouse to join you there for drinks. But she's incredulous: "What the hell?! You *promised* to pick up dinner on the way home, but once again completely forgot—even after that big conversation about needing to be more attentive to the family's needs." This scenario doesn't have a happy ending, either.

The malleability of boundaries between work and home is particularly problematic if you work out of your home. The kids can't tear around yelling their heads off when you're trying to call investors. Your spreadsheets and product samples may wind up decorating every surface in the house, and you may put a lot of wear and tear on the family car driving from one appointment to the next. Your family may not feel that you're working from home, but that they're living in your office.

When Charles Chang launched Vega, he worked from a home office because he thought it would give him more family time. But while he was present in body, his spirit was somewhere else entirely. "When I was home I was never really *home*," Charles says. After a few years, his wife kindly but firmly encouraged him to create better boundaries between work life and home life by getting a new office. Outside the family's home.

Supporting an entrepreneur is not all that easy. A big reason is that we don't struggle with relinquishing control just in our work lives. We've also got a problem with that at home. So not only do we tend to demand a lot from our partners; we can also be a tad controlling, or so they tell us. It's an occupational hazard: you're so accustomed to being independent in your work that it's not so easy to morph into an accommodating, meet-you-halfway partner at home. Compromise just feels less efficient, somehow. *I mean, it's my job to come up with the best, most expedient solution—so why waste time listening to your ideas and beating about the bush with all this touchy-feely stuff?* I doubt many entrepreneurs would phrase it quite like that. But most of us do act that way at home—at least some of the time. We're used to calling the shots, and that bossiness bleeds over into our personal relationships, too.

Natasha Vandenhurk struggles with checking her natural tendencies at the door. The minute she arrives home, she makes supper and then finds something to clean. She's the type who likes to finish what she starts—that kind of doggedness works well for her at work. But at home, where there's always something new to clean and straighten up, it means that it takes her forever to unwind. Being driven also makes her hard to live with, sometimes. "When you take that drive that you put into your business and apply it at home, you can push your spouse too hard," she acknowledges. "I always want it done *now*. He doesn't."

The very traits that make you successful can take a real toll on your marriage. Remember Greg Chamandy, co-founder of Gildan Activewear? More recently, Greg and his wife Chantal acquired Liquid Nutrition. Greg asked Chantal to name the hardest thing about living with him, and she didn't hesitate: stubbornness. He agrees. "Once I have a focus and commitment to something, it's hard to get me off it," he says. However, he points out that the trait has always worked well for him.

Spouses and Other Strangers

If I had to name the single biggest threat to an entrepreneur's marriage, it would be absence. Much of the time, you'll simply be missing in action. I don't just mean you'll be putting in long hours—lots of senior executives do that. I'm talking about the fact that even when you schedule quality couple time and keep the commitment, you may be unable to stop your brain from working on a job problem. Your body's present, but your mind is elsewhere.

Try to imagine what it's like for your partner to witness the powerful hold your business has on you. You appear to think of little else, day and night. Many spouses of entrepreneurs feel they just can't compete. They have to go all out to command more than a sliver of your attention. No wonder they so frequently talk about feeling "abandoned" and "betrayed." From their perspective, you really are having a love affair. And you're being flagrant about it!

The intense emotional connection you feel toward your business may quickly be matched by an equally intense emotional response from your spouse: resentment. *Why do I have to wait in line to get your attention?* If you go to an event together, your partner is unlikely to view it as a date. *There's just no escaping the business.* If you need time alone to recharge one evening, your spouse may be hurt or angry. *Why do you have time and energy for everybody else? What about us? What about me?*

There's a scarcity of statistics about entrepreneurship and divorce, but I'm willing to bet that the divorce rate is much higher for entrepreneurs. Even if spousal neglect doesn't take a marriage down, having increasingly separate lives and divergent goals may do the trick. If entrepreneurs aren't careful, along with a business venture they may create a "toxic cocktail of resentment and anxiety," warns Meg Cadoux Hirshberg, particularly if the family's financial security is placed at risk. She writes a terrific column for *Inc.* on what it's like to be married to an entrepreneur, and she knows what she's talking about: her husband is Gary Hirshberg, co-founder of Stonyfield Yogurt, one of the leading yogurt manufacturers in the United States. Their marriage is still going strong, though Cadoux Hirshberg writes that they've survived periods of "distance and suffocating tension" directly caused by the lifestyle. She points out that marriage is supposed to be about shared interests, but entrepreneurs are fundamentally doing their own thing—and are enraptured by it. "How often have you heard an entrepreneur describe her company as her 'passion'? How often have you heard one say the same about her spouse?" she asks, rhetorically.

If a marriage is strained *before* an entrepreneur decides to go for it, the relationship is almost certainly doomed. No marriage counsellor in the world would advise a couple with a troubled relationship to increase the financial stress on their relationship and spend even less quality time together.

Business success, too, can spell trouble for a marriage. Success doesn't necessarily make entrepreneurs more relaxed or more attentive and considerate. Quite the opposite, in some cases. Yung Wu has watched a lot of entrepreneurs go through IPOs and says that in some cases, the "self-absorption component" of the entrepreneur is so high, the person turns into the kind of raging egomaniac who "sucks all the oxygen out of a room." It wasn't a stretch for him to imagine that these people would also suck all the oxygen out of their relationships, too. "I think with any rela-tionship . . . whether it's with a friend or spouse, you have to make sure you put a few deposits in before you withdraw. That's just common sense," says Yung, "but it's not common sense for a lot of entrepreneurs I've observed."

The problem, of course, is that you need a ramped-up inter-nal belief system to get the job done, but from there it's only a short hop to becoming a legend in your own mind. Unless you balance your self-regard with a sense of humour about yourself, you'll almost certainly fly blind into one of those relationship red zones I alluded to earlier. If you don't heed the sirens, you may come home one day to find your spouse at the door, bags packed.

This is a more common scenario than you might think. Many

of my friends who are entrepreneurs have been blindsided by divorce. They truly never saw it coming. Their spouses were telling other people, "He's never home. The business always comes first. I'm last on his list." Yet the entrepreneurs were saying things like, "I love my life. It's perfect!"

So they're shocked to discover things didn't look quite so perfect from the other side of the bed. Yet I'm convinced that sadly many of them, if they'd been forced to choose, would have chosen the business over the marriage. In essence, that's what they were doing every day. Ultimatums just don't work very well with entrepreneurs, because of our need to feel in charge. "A hundred-million-dollar deal I can control. Even if it fails, I can fix it. It's manageable," explains Tony Lacavera. A woman who tries to make him toe a certain line causes him way more stress. When he's dating someone, he tells her, "You will have total control of our relationship if you give up total control of me. I am so happy to go and meet your friends for dinner, drinks, whatever, but if I'm an hour late and you give me grief . . ." He told me that he has a visceral response when someone tries to curb his independence. "When I feel like I'm not being trusted or I'm being asked to report in on something, it's over. I get increasingly defensive and build an increasingly strong set of walls around me. It winds up having the opposite effect."

If ultimatums don't work, and if some of the problems I've described are simply inevitable conditions of entrepreneurial life, how can you live your dream without losing your marriage? I've been divorced twice, so I recognize my credibility may not be intact on this issue. But I think the key is to understand what you're *both* getting into. If you're asking a spouse to get on the roller coaster with you, you do need to have some understanding what the ride will feel like for him—and some empathy, too, when it's particularly harrowing. You're not the only one who's under stress, and also not the only one who's being expected to survive and thrive. Feeling that you're in this together—and then reminding yourself of that fact every day—is a very good first step in divorce-proofing your marriage.

Before you strike out for independence, you need to have a serious conversation with your significant other about how life will change for you both. So much of the resentment that builds in these situations is preventable if you know what you can reasonably expect of each other. But even if you have an extremely supportive spouse, don't expect a walk in the park. Natasha has just such a husband, but she thinks that even he sometimes feels like an unpaid employee. "He has his limits, too. I need to be aware of that. I am looking for one hundred percent support . . . on an unlimited basis, but . . . he's entitled to his own time."

After she made her *Dragons' Den* pitch, Natasha had to work late every night, so her husband made dinner all week. When Friday rolled around, she called him to say she'd pick up groceries on the way home and make dinner. He replied, "Yeah, you know what? I'd be really happy if you'd make supper tonight." She knew by the tone of his voice that it was a good thing she'd made that call—she knew he'd reached his limit. "We just went to bed in silence. But then we woke up and it was a new day and we worked it through."

Learning how to navigate your relationships will be a work in progress, just like learning how to run a company. The main lesson I've learned over the years is that you can't expect everyone around you to be as passionate about your business as you are. I have to remind myself that this is *my* dream, and it's unfair of me to expect others even to understand fully, much less share, the depth of my devotion. However, I can help them to understand the reality of my life—both what they have every right to expect from me, and what they just have to accept about my life. Some things I can't change: the unpredictability of my schedule, for instance, and the fact that the phone is always going to ring. Of course, I don't always have to answer it, and that's something I've learned the hard way.

Some spouses decide that the best way to protect themselves from the ups and downs of your life is simply not to hear about them. That's what Meg Cadoux Hirshberg, the *Inc.* columnist, decided would work for her. She just couldn't take hearing about Stonyfield Yogurt all the time, especially when the topic of conversation was her family's potential financial ruin. So for about five years, her husband was under strict instructions not to tell her all the ins and outs of what was going on at the company. He didn't mention how much her own mother had invested in the business; and during the year the business was losing about $25,000 a week, he kept quiet about that. Nor did he make a peep when they opened a new production facility and, at the end of the first week, were forced to throw out 75 percent of the yogurt because it failed to meet quality standards. "It was terrifying," he told a reporter in 2012. "But also, it was embarrassing. It was a reflection on me. I don't think I wanted her to know that her husband was failing again." Eventually, when the business was on surer footing, she reversed her don't-ask, don't-tell policy. But, Gary Hirshberg points out, it worked well for *both* of them during the years they observed it, "because it meant home was a place I could escape to from work, and I wasn't burdening her with problems." He recognized that she already had plenty, simply because she was married to an entrepreneur.

The Practically Perfect Entrepreneurial Partner

So what kind of person is the ideal significant other for an entrepreneur? Greg Chamandy, of Gildan Activewear, says it's someone who understands that when you're starting out, you'll be burning the candle at both ends, and is willing to invest in the journey along with you. "Someone who wants you to be home for supper at 5 o'clock is going to be a problem," he adds. Chris Emery, of OMG Candy, says an entrepreneur needs a partner who's kind, patient, forgiving, and believes in him, like his wife, Carol.

Natasha Vandenhurk figures an entrepreneur's spouse needs to have "a multitude of traits." He has to be secure as a person and in his work. He has to understand she's not a whirling dervish on purpose; she's working at high pitch so much because the business demands it. He should be someone more laid-back than she is so he will rein her in at times. And he should be willing to pitch in. Fortunately, her husband, Lane Fitzsimmons, an electrical engineer whose schedule is a little more predictable, fits the bill nicely on all counts.

What traits should set off alarm bells? Wayne Fromm says he doesn't do well with a high-maintenance partner. She needs to be secure enough to be okay with his need for "alone time." I certainly know where he's coming from on that score. My job is social 24/7, so I crave solitude the way other people crave sleep. I need it to refuel; otherwise, I feel depleted. The need is most intense after a period of being in the public eye. I feel blessed to have the show and the opportunities that come with it. And I do enjoy meeting with, learning from, and giving to people. (When I was little, I wanted to be an actress or a social worker, so I guess I found the perfect career to channel both desires.) But in the end, you have only so much emotional capital to go around.

I think most people who draw on their creativity for a living really need solitude. If you're always channelling your inner muse, or your work demands that you to be "on" a lot, at some point you will need to restore. Wayne tells a story that wonderfully illustrates this point. Some years ago, he says, a friend of his was jogging on the Beltline Trail in Toronto when he ran past a guy sitting on a bench. The guy was a dead ringer for Mick Jagger. The Rolling Stones were living in the city at the time, rehearsing for one of their tours—maybe it really *was* Mick? The jogger ran back to the bench and asked. "Are you who I think you are?" The man replied, "Not today."

Whether the story's apocryphal or not, I love its message: creative, entrepreneurial individuals—even the most famous and exhibitionistic among them—need time to themselves. If that sounds like you, then it's probably a good idea to have a partner who understands your need for alone time, whether you spend it running or curling up with a good book. People who are themselves naturally independent are most likely to understand perfectly and not view your need for solitude as a form of rejection.

That is why I think self-reliance is the most important quality an entrepreneur needs in a partner. You want someone who knows how to find his own fulfillment in life, someone who's willing to take responsibility for his own happiness and is not constantly looking to you to provide it. I know of one successful entrepreneurial marriage, for instance, where the wife is a marathon runner. She spends a great deal of time training. And when she runs a race, her husband, the entrepreneur, is always there to cheer her on. Both of them know in their bones what it means to have a driving passion and goal. Since they both intuitively understand that desire, it's much easier for them to honour it in each other.

Two for the Road

Entrepreneurs' marriages come in many varieties. There isn't one recipe for success, but a few tried-and-true models. Sometimes the spouse functions as a gatekeeper/power-behind-the-throne type, and finds a way to accompany the entrepreneur on the journey. If the spouse has the interest, aptitude, and skill set to be a gatekeeper, he—or more often, she—can wind up in a position of real power in the company. Both people feel they are partners in the same venture, contributing in different ways but both essential to success.

I once heard an entrepreneur use a movie analogy to describe an entrepreneurial marriage, and it stayed with me. The idea is that the couple is shooting a movie together. The entrepreneur is the star, and the spouse has a supporting role. Sure, the star attracts the financing and attention, but the movie can't get made without a strong supporting cast and crew, and the star won't shine without them. It's a collaborative exercise. The other option is that both partners are starring in their own movies and, in that case, need to hire two supporting casts.

Yung and Katrina Wu's marriage, his second, seems like a very modern variation on this model. Yung and his first wife, who was training to become an opera singer, met and married while they were both still in university. While Yung thinks that marrying young probably contributed to their split, which occurred six years after he launched his first company, he believes the entrepreneurial lifestyle had something to do with it, too. "Between the time allocation of growing a business and the adrenaline rush of seeing it become successful, one thing leads to another and it becomes a bit of a recursive loop. A lot of my energy went from the relationship into the business," he explains.

However, his wife was also on a one-way street, headed in the opposite direction. She was similarly focused on her singing career. "It's way too hard to have two people with priorities like that," Yung says now. He realized that he had to have a different kind of partner, one who wasn't as hyper-focused on her own career as he is on his. Now, Katrina is plenty focused. Although she calls herself a dilettante, she has, among other things, studied linguistics and worked as a diplomat, sommelier, writer, teacher, and florist. When Yung met her, "she was about to move to Hawaii, grow orchids, and write her next book." But though she's highly accomplished, Katrina takes her measure less from her career than from the interesting experiences and people in her life. At the moment, her driving passion is a cause the couple shares: *Different Is Cool*, a digital magazine (which she's editing) and social enterprise foundation they've launched to celebrate and encourage young "outliers, creatives and originals" to follow their convictions and find their own path. (Songwriter Daniel Lanois and author Margaret Atwood are two of its "Patrons of Cool.") Yung loves working with young entrepreneurs because they haven't yet learned they might fail at something. "They're full of great energy and ideas." And that's what Katrina brings to their relationship, too.

His wife, says Yung, "understands that we're in this together. She knows that our future is linked to the initiatives I'm driving." Therefore, although he still keeps crazy hours, she's "unbelievably supportive," and they design their lives around his schedule. They also decided not to have children, so they have the freedom to take off for Mexico or go for a long motorcycle ride when the opportunity arises. They're both able to be flexible enough with their work to take advantage of those opportunities.

But Katrina plays another role for Yung as well. During his

darkest hours at Castek, when he was laying off close friends and fending off financial ruin, she was there to support him emotionally at the end of every day. She's still there, and he still needs it at times. "Two, maybe three times a year, when I know that I am a complete fraud, that I have done a fantastic job of fooling everybody around me, and I totally lose my confidence in myself, she always reminds me that, 'No, you've earned every single grey hair you have; and every decision you make, you should honour.' She always reminds me, 'You're going to get through this.' She's my rock."

In most of the entrepreneurial relationships I've observed where the spouse is playing a supporting or gatekeeping role, the entrepreneur is male. It's worth noting the paradox: straight guys who embrace a non-traditional career path nevertheless often lean toward pretty traditional marriages. Relationships where the woman is the entrepreneur and the male partner takes more of a back-seat role remain few and far between, in my experience. But happy relationships like Annette Verschuren's marriage give me hope.

Male entrepreneurs still have an easier time finding practical help and emotional support in one package. The simple explanation is that women remain much more comfortable with the notion of a man supporting them than men are with the reverse. Yes, things are slowly changing, but you have to be an extremely confident person to be willing to flip roles and be comfortable with the idea of thumbing your nose at deeply entrenched social expectations.

Can you be a successful entrepreneur if you're not in a relationship? Sure, just as you can be happy when you're single and live alone. But are you better off if you have support? Probably. My life would certainly be easier and more enjoyable if I had someone to help organize it, to travel with me, and to be there at the end of the day. Whose wouldn't?

Is it likely to happen? Well, maybe I'm just having a delusionally optimistic entrepreneurial moment, but I still believe it's possible.

Two Entrepreneurs, One Address

What happens when you have two entrepreneurs with full-blown careers living under the same roof? Is the marriage destined for trouble? Not necessarily. It can actually be a real advantage to live with someone who intuitively understands the lifestyle because he's living it, too. Certainly, he's going to be much more likely to cut you slack when you explain that instead of celebrating your anniversary, you're going to be pitching a new client.

In Chapter 7, I told you about Samantha Reynolds working pretty much flat out for eight years before she decided the time was right to try to incorporate leisure into her life. However, she had to look beyond her home to figure out how to do that, because her partner, Pete McCormack, is a writer and filmmaker who's as into his work as she is. Leisure was not in his vocabulary, either. Now married, with a three-year-old son, the couple has taken only one holiday in the eight years they've been together. But that's never been a bone of contention between them. Samantha figures she'd be under more pressure to take time off if her husband had a job with regimented vacation time. "We're not exactly role models for each other," she points out, "when it comes to taking time off."

When Samantha decided to "explore what it felt like not to be a workaholic," she did finally find greater equilibrium. Yet she also concluded that being a workaholic wasn't so bad. She saw how happily and endlessly her husband worked, and realized that "some people can go full tilt in one area of their lives and be happy." Tina Fey would certainly agree. She recently said, "I have no hobbies. I don't scrapbook. There's just work and children, and work and children. What else do you need?"

Samantha thinks being married to someone who is also "all in" as an entrepreneur has had two dominant effects on their relationship. On the upside, their individual need to chart their own course connects them at an elemental level. However, though her tendency to distance herself from feeling uncertain or fearful is an asset for an entrepreneur, she thinks it may not be such a great thing in a marriage. "There are advantages to thinking positively, but there's also a great strength in just allowing yourself to feel vulnerable," she explains. "Pete and I have a wonderful marriage. He's my favourite person in the whole world, and my very, very best friend. But if there's an area we can work on, that would be it."

What About the Kids?

Where do the kids fit in? What's it like for them to live with a parent who's an entrepreneur? How is it possible, for that matter, to have this lifestyle and still be a good parent? Well, I think the first order of business is recognizing that, in an essential way, your children aren't just your dependants. They're your partners, too. I didn't come to this realization until I was much older, but the truth is that my kids and I built Venture *together*.

The company is our joint achievement because it was built on their sacrifices as much as mine. They gave at the blood bank, as they'd be the first to tell you. They love talking about how they had to ride around on those office dollies while all their friends were playing in the park. If I'd taken them to the park or been a soccer mom or participated in the PTA like their friends' moms, I could not have built my company. It simply wouldn't have happened. When you work for somebody else, even if you're deeply committed to your job, you simply don't have the same emotional investment in your work. When you're not all in, you can draw a line. But when you are, as I was, your kids are in the position of competing for as much of your time, energy, and emotional bandwidth as they can possibly get. If you're a single parent with four kids and you're working the kind of hours I was, let's be honest: there's very little emotional bandwidth available.

Sometimes I felt like an eagle—touching down in their lives, then taking off again. We all paid a price for that, in terms of lost opportunities. It didn't help that I didn't know anybody else who was working the kinds of hours I did. People always imagine the freedom they'll have as entrepreneurs, but in many ways I think of those early years as a time of never-ending sacrifice for us all.

I think my kids wish I'd been around more. But even though they didn't get a whole lot of face time with me growing up, their childhood wasn't just about what they had to give up. It was also about what they had the opportunity to observe. They saw the value of effort. They saw that you really can build something from nothing. They saw that if you dream big and work hard, you can overcome daunting obstacles and change your life. In a visceral way, that has served them well as adults because they understand what independence really means.

I think growing up as they did affected all four of them in different ways, and, of course, I can't say how they'd be different had they grown up in different circumstances. But I do believe the experience has taught them a great deal about taking risks, solving problems, and surviving hardships. It has certainly taught them the value and necessity of self-reliance.

When you're so busy managing a business and making lunches and trying to get everybody to school on time, the moments just fly by. I wish I'd been a little more present in the moment with my children, the way I had to be with my business. And I wish I'd figured that out a lot earlier. But my children are the people they are at least partly because I'm an entrepreneur. I am super proud of how they have turned out and who they are, and I feel grateful that they are proud of what I've accomplished instead of resentful of the price they paid for it. Somehow, amid all the challenges and chaos, I must have done something right, because they definitely know who they are to me: the loves of my life.

Chapter 10

The Relationship Conundrum

There's no point in soft-pedalling this, so I'm just going to give it to you straight: entrepreneurs, as a group, can be not very good at relationships with significant others. There are exceptions, of course, and perhaps you're one of them. But many entrepreneurs are single and just can't seem to make a relationship work. Others are trying, but . . . it's an uphill battle, especially for their partners. Still others have tales of woe about their romantic misadventures, or a divorce—or two—under their belts. In fact, we have such a lousy track record, collectively, that I don't think it would be even slightly controversial to suggest that having a happy, fulfilling relationship is the toughest challenge of the entrepreneurial lifestyle.

That's true for many people, entrepreneurs or not. Having it all is difficult even for someone with a traditional job and a conventional lifestyle. But when you're an entrepreneur, the normal difficulties and pressures are multiplied exponentially. The crux of the matter is this: many entrepreneurs, of both genders, behave as though they find their businesses sexier and more interesting than their significant others. Maybe that's not how entrepreneurs actually feel in their hearts, but I'm talking about behaviour, and how that behaviour is perceived by the person on the receiving end. The significant other often feels, well, insignificant. Many say they feel almost as though the entrepreneur in their lives is having an affair. The fact that the affair is with a business enterprise doesn't reduce the pain. It hurts to know that the person you're with is clearly capable of single-minded devotion—just, not to you. It doesn't feel good to look across the table and see someone who's starry-eyed—only, not about you. Feeling neglected and overlooked feels crummy, and at a certain point it doesn't matter whether the rival is a business or a person.

The irony here is that the same traits that make entrepreneurs good at business are exactly the ones that make them lousy at love. Entrepreneurs tend to be focused, driven, impatient, perennially distracted people who are prone to interrupting and have a hard time slowing down to talk about anything other than The Business—all of which works well in the business world, of course, but wouldn't look so good in a personal ad. Picture it: "Bossy control freak with no free time seeks significant other." Would you even honestly be interested in the human doormat who'd respond to such an ad?

Me neither. And yet, it's so easy to treat our significant others this way. The first time you hear your partner complain about your supposed selfishness, you may be shell-shocked. Okay, I wasn't the most attentive person in the world, but come on. It was never all about me—I was building this for us and our family! But, of course, your company is an extension of who you are. It is, in a very fundamental way, all about you. You thought you were focusing on your company; the other person thought you were focusing on yourself. You're both right.

Most entrepreneurs honestly believe they are looking for a relationship of equals. And in theory, it's true. But reality is different. The average entrepreneur is used to being the Decider-in-Chief, the person who calls the shots, the person who believes that compromise is for wimps. That's how we got our businesses off the ground: we refused to compromise on our vision. That stubbornness and unwillingness to compromise was rewarded and reinforced. Many of us have difficulty switching it off in our relationships, which are, of course, all about compromising and finding a middle way and figuring out how to make tough decisions together.

I can't pretend to know what the solutions are. What I do know is that the entrepreneurial lifestyle can be extremely hard on our partners, especially if we're perennially in crisis mode. If they see that the only way to get our attention is to yell "Fire!" they're likely to become serial arsonists. Carving out couple time, and trying to make sure you spend it doing something other than talking about business, is obviously key. But making another person feel like a priority doesn't require grand displays or epic date nights. It can be as simple as running out to get her a latte in the morning; daily acts of thoughtfulness have a cumulative effect, and will buy you a lot of forgiveness when you drop the ball on other things. To know which gestures will mean the most to your partner, though, you do need some baseline level of intimacy. Which leads me to another fundamental problem: intimacy is something that can really scare entrepreneurs, because it's inherently risky.

Tolerate Risks? Are You Nuts?

It's not possible to have an intimate relationship with another adult unless you're willing to take emotional risks. Great news, right? Comfort with risk-taking is in our DNA. Well, yes and no: I know entrepreneurs who will bet the farm and everything on it with much greater confidence and ease than they will risk feeling even slightly vulnerable in a relationship. I recognize that split in myself, too, and I've come to believe that it's fundamental to our makeup as entrepreneurs. In fact, it may well be the central paradox of the entrepreneurial personality. That's why I believe that gaining an understanding of the complicated relationship so many entrepreneurs have with risk is a vital step for anyone thinking of becoming an entrepreneur—or considering loving or living with one.

Many wheeler-dealers find relationship pressures far more stressful than any they have to contend with in their business lives. Certainly that's true of me. I routinely take flyers that look crazy from the outside, investing in start-ups that are the opposite of a sure thing, but that doesn't stress me out. It's worth mentioning that these kinds of business risks often have mucky emotional repercussions: there can be conflict, anger, hurt feelings if things don't work out.

In a business venture, I'm all in. I'll put money and time on the line, knowing I might lose one or both, but fortunately I can always make more money and find more time. In a romantic relationship, the only thing I have to put on the line is myself. And I do. One hundred and fifty percent. When it comes to love, I'm as passionate and fully committed as I am in business. My relationships consume me and, because they do, more often than not they scare me, too. Because the practical, survival side of me isn't totally keen to risk the only chip I have.

The truth is that as entrepreneurs we've had to forge emotional armour to protect ourselves from the slings and arrows of the business world, but that armour is no help at all in the romantic arena. In fact, it's a problem. There, you have to be prepared to let down your defences, or what's the point? The whole idea is to let someone get close enough to know you—which means, close enough to hurt you. And the thought of willingly ceding control to someone else in that way is very difficult for the average entrepreneur. The thing is, we know we can rely on ourselves. We're independent. The prospect of being interdependent can feel like a threat to the very core of our identity.

A related issue: after taking that risk and revealing yourself, what do you do if the relationship isn't working? Some entrepreneurs told me it seemed there was only one possible solution: stay, and fix it. After all, that's what we do when we encounter problems in our businesses. We're fixers and problem-solvers, and tend to believe that where there's a will, there's a way. We've surmounted huge obstacles in business even when all hope seemed lost, so surely we can surmount whatever's wrong with this relationship.

"Fixing" is our default command, and accepting that it doesn't help in certain situations may require repeated botched fixes. Annette Verschuren, for instance, admits that she always knew by the six-month mark whether a relationship was going anywhere, yet she also hung on, trying to make it work, long after that. She used the approach that had always been successful in her work life: "I take that cat home and it's forlorn and I try to fix it," is how she puts it. But no matter how diligently she tried, it failed to do the trick. She couldn't fix a relationship because it wasn't just up to her.

My friend Margot Micallef, founder and CEO of Oliver Capital Partners Inc., a private equity investment/advisory firm, did something similar. She was a big believer in "the greatness within people," and she used to think it took only her own sheer willpower to bring that out—she has a great track record for inspiring people at work. But she's realized that in a relationship, her own willpower sometimes isn't enough. What matters is not just what she sees in another person, but what he sees in himself.

The good news is that Annette and Margot are proof that it's possible to learn when to hold and when to fold in relationships. This is not a gender issue, by the way. It's an entrepreneurial issue, and one that many men also have. Tony Lacavera, for instance, has the same "risk-tolerant in business/risk-averse in romance" dichotomy that I do. He told me that when he was in the throes of the CRTC hearings, while the big three wireless titans were disputing his right to enter their domain and provide an alternative service, he actually relished the proceedings. When the other side showed up flanked by lawyers and armed with reams of data, he knew they were scared, so he figured he must be doing something right. His company was hemorrhaging capital at the time, but he wasn't worried: whatever the outcome, he knew he'd find a solution. What he was really worried about, what stressed him out most during that time period, was his uncertainty about where things stood with his then long-time girlfriend (they eventually split up).

His mother didn't understand this at all. "How can you not feel pressured with $1.8 billion over your head?" she asked. Tony's answer: "Because I can fix it. It's manageable—even if it fails."

Relationships are not so easily fixed, because it doesn't all come down to you. It's not a dictatorship; it's a democracy where people can vote with their feet. Tony wanted his mother to understand that relationships are the only things in life that make him feel unhappy, anxious, or pressured. But she drew a slightly different moral from his story: "You're brilliant, you created all this from nothing, but you are a complete moron when it comes to anything to do with women!"

Dealing with the Double Standard

Successful entrepreneurs of the female persuasion don't lack for love: we love our work. It doesn't just pay the rent. It sustains us. Work is where we turn for our kicks, our sense of identity, and much of our emotional fulfillment. Some of us would also like to find romantic love—someone to pat us on the back now and then, lean on when times are tough, and help keep us grounded. But we're not interested in being defined by a relationship. And we don't want one at any cost. What turns our heads? Confidence, strength, and character, for starters. Independence: financial and emotional. An individual with his own passions and pursuits. We're not interested in needy. But we'd also like someone who can keep up, or at least who won't squawk about the pace we keep. A tall order? Perhaps. But we set the bar high in business. Why settle for less in love?

And yet, for female entrepreneurs, success can be a double-edged sword. On one level, it's a numbers game. Once you've reached a certain age and level of success, the pool of date-worthy candidates is just much smaller, and you may be competing not only with younger women but against your own success. Some men are confident enough not to view a woman's success as a threat but, in my experience, more are just not comfortable with the idea of making less money, say, or having less recognition. They find it a turnoff. So you may start to feel you're being penalized for your success, and that feels particularly unfair given that success heightens the sex appeal of male entrepreneurs. But the same traits that work like catnip on women—drive, persistence, killer instinct—can send men running for the hills. I'm often told—and have heard from other successful single woman—that men find the combination of success, intelligence, and beauty very intimidating. That's ironic because in a man's case, it's a recipe for a total find.

Social media expert Mari Smith is no stranger to the success-as-liability conundrum. A well-known trainer and author in the online marketing world, Mari earns a good portion of her income as an international speaker. The events she speaks at are often filled with eligible partners, many of whom are dying to speak to the six-foot blonde but too intimidated to ask for her number.

"Most people are either intimidated or assume I must be married or have a partner, so they just don't bother asking," Mari says.

Of course, powerful women in every field confront this double standard, but apparently the E-word has pretty much the same effect on men that waving a cross does on vampires. In one of Meg Cadoux Hirshberg's *Inc.* columns on the romantic lives of single and divorced female entrepreneurs, she recounted the experience of a divorced CEO who posted an online dating profile that didn't get a nibble when she identified herself as an entrepreneur. After she removed that one noun, responses streamed in.

Cadoux Hirshberg discovered that some men simply didn't take a woman who ran her own business seriously, and therefore grew impatient with her devotion to it. One female CEO noted wryly, "When a guy owns a business, people think he's Mark Zuckerberg. A woman says she owns her own business, and people think she's stringing beads in her basement." Another strike against female entrepreneurs is that their hours are so unpredictable. But here's the real sucker punch: while potential investors are hesitant to invest in female entrepreneurs' ventures for fear that they'll focus too much on hearth and home, some prospective boyfriends worry they'll do just the opposite.

Women who are in the spotlight have an additional disadvantage: they need a partner who's comfortable in his own skin, has his own thing going on, or has arrived at a place in life where he's fine with playing a behind-the-scenes role. That's a hard enough role for a woman to play for a man, let alone for a man to play for a woman. Jann Arden points out that it's particularly tough for a partner to stand by mutely when a throng of adoring fans suddenly materializes. "Whoever you're with has got to be incredibly strong and secure and realize that this is just part of what you do," she says. But even the strongest, most secure men may tire of playing the Prince Philip role. On some level, no matter how happy you are together, it's got to be a drag sometimes when the mortal, flawed woman you know is treated as an idol.

Given all this, it's not surprising that many successful female CEOs consider it more rewarding to invest in a pursuit with a greater return on investment: our work. Whether we find love or not, whether love flourishes or fades, we'll always have our work, and our love for it never falters. Along with our kids, our family and friends, and our recreational and charitable activities, work provides us with our deepest emotional sustenance and greatest sense of control. And in many ways, work seems like a higher calling. Men, of course, have long defined themselves by their work. For the first time in history, though, women are starting to do that, too.

I'm all for finding fulfillment and self-actualization at work. But I don't think happiness at work precludes being in an emotionally fulfilling relationship. In my view, true happiness comes when you take a 360-degree view of your life and aim to be fulfilled in all areas of it—especially in your relationships.

I've had successes and failures in both my business life and my private life. When I fail in business I always try to figure out what I did that contributed to the problem. And even though it's a heck of a lot harder and more confusing, I do the exact same thing when a personal relationship ends. By reflecting on failed personal relationships I've learned, for instance, that because I fall in love hard and give my relationships everything I have, I begin to feel off balance and painfully vulnerable when we've reached a certain level of intimacy. So I pull back to a safer distance—usually by focusing on my work—a habit that has been the downfall of more than one relationship. I'm not proud of it, but I'm aware of it. And just like I won't let myself make the same mistake in business once I'm aware of what I did wrong, I'm committed to not letting my fear of vulnerability sabotage my next relationship.

Call me a hopeless romantic, but I still believe a long-term relationship is possible and is going to be a part of my life. And I'm willing to do the personal work required to make it happen.

My friend Margot Micallef is a great source of inspiration for me here. She had a few lean years during which she had a hard time finding a partner. Being a goal-oriented sort, a few years ago she followed a friend's suggestion to make a list of the top 100 things she wanted in a man. "I actually wrote down 104 things because I'm an overachiever," she says. "Financially secure" was one of her top three must-haves. The others? "Kindness" and "a man, not a boy." She got all three, "and then some," when her friends set her up with another entrepreneur. They're now engaged.

When You're Together in Business and in Bed

When business partners *are* married, the arrangement comes with a whole other level of complexity. Some husband-and-wife teams have great success, while others fail miserably. My own experience falls into the latter category. When I brought my then husband into my business, it didn't work out. Looking back, I brought him in for all the wrong reasons, but I didn't see that at the time.

My ex was an analytical kind of guy, much more of a process person than I am. He convinced me that the business needed more of what he had to offer and less of my style. He led me to believe that he'd add more value than I was adding in that role. But to be honest, I also wanted to please him. So my decision to make him the president was driven by both business and personal reasons. Right from the start, I blurred those boundaries.

And once he took over that role, I couldn't let go because I knew I had done it for the wrong reasons. I had a different view of how to run the company than he did, which created tensions between us at work, and they spilled over at home. Eventually there was no refuge. I think you can probably imagine how awful it was, for both of us. I'd wanted to make him happy, and yet having him in that role didn't make me happy.

I'd dealt with many challenges as an entrepreneur, but the emotional turmoil I experienced during that time was by far the most difficult challenge I have ever faced. I felt profoundly isolated. I couldn't complain to employees about my own husband. And I couldn't turn to my husband to vent or to get support.

When you partner with a spouse, it gets messy when you decide it's time to part ways. Really messy. You're entangled emotionally *and* financially, both at home and at work. You're trying to get disentangled and protect your business and carry on as a leader, but you're utterly emotionally distracted. And even though you're no longer living together, you still have to see each other at the office every day. It takes time to get through all this. In our case, a couple of years, and they were very tough ones all the way around.

After our divorce, I went to Thailand for a month on my own. I was 50 at that point, and it was and still is the only time in my life when I have taken such significant time away from work. I needed to rediscover who I was and rethink what I wanted in life, and I knew I had to get as far away as possible for that to happen. Now, I didn't let go entirely. There's no force in the world, not even my own unhappiness, that's powerful enough to pry my BlackBerry from my hand. I still worked remotely every day, but the distance was exactly what I needed to get my thoughts and feelings straight and move forward. Going away at that particular juncture was also the right decision for my business. Being a little more hands-off didn't hurt anything in the long run, and stabilizing myself emotionally was the key to re-establishing my new president's and my combined leadership of the company.

I realized that I should have been more assertive in acting on my view of what was in the company's best interests. I knew what I had to do, but I just didn't have enough faith in myself to act. The good news is that I learned from the experience. These days, when I'm facing decisions that have personal as well as professional ramifications, I know to project into the future and think long and hard about how my decision today might harm the business down the road. I'm much more purposeful about such matters now, and I've learned not to lead with my heart. My gut instincts are the ones I should trust.

Finding a New Way

I've been married twice—three times if you count being married to my work. Any marriage is hard work, but I've found that the long hours of building my businesses are a lot less scary than the loss of control I sometimes feel in romantic relationships.

For a long time, I thought I was the only person who felt this way, and I viewed it as a character flaw. But as I talked to entrepreneurs across the country about the defining elements of the lifestyle, I realized something: it's not just me. Many of them feel the same way, and they refuse to feel guilty about it. Maybe the traits that help us achieve success are wired in so deeply that it's just not possible to check them at the door when entering a relationship—and now, I no longer wish I could. I wouldn't be me anymore.

Tony Lacavera has reached a similar conclusion. Now in his late 30s, he'd love to find a life partner and have kids, but he thinks successful relationships are the exception, not the rule, for high-powered entrepreneurs. He freely admits that his own have been less than stellar, despite sincerely trying to make a go of it. After one girlfriend told him he was already married—to his mission—he made a real effort to fight that tendency within himself. Finally, he realized he wasn't being true to himself. Rather, he was trying to live up to a societal standard he didn't even agree with. Why should he have to apologize for loving his work with a passion? In no other area of his life does he feel bound by traditional ways of looking at the world—if he had, he couldn't have taken on the giants in the telecommunications industry.

Embracing alternative ways of living and recalibrating personal goals is exactly what many other entrepreneurs are choosing to do, too. Just as they flouted conventional notions about doing business, they're reinventing their own ideas about what they want their lives to look like.

Take Diana Olsen of Balzac's Coffee, who was "taking a break" from dating when we spoke. Diana has been married, but she never had a burning desire to be a mother—until she hit 40 and began to think about adopting a child. She had no shortage of reasons to talk herself out of it. *It will take too long. It will be hard being a single parent.* But neither prospect seemed as daunting as the regret she might experience later if she didn't do it, so she decided she'd just jump in. "You only get this life," she said. "I knew if I just did it I would never regret it." And she hasn't. Six-year-old Annabelle, whom she adopted as a newborn, is clearly the love of her life. "I have an amazing, beautiful, healthy daughter. It's the story of my life that I'm the most proud of, more than Balzac."

One high-octane male entrepreneur I know is also mulling over the idea of adopting a child on his own. He thinks being a single parent might actually mesh well with his entrepreneurial lifestyle: he can afford to have a lot of support around him, and his schedule is flexible enough for him to spend a lot of time with a child. What he wants in his life is more love. Maybe, he figures, he's been going about it all wrong. Maybe he'd be happier skipping dates altogether and focusing instead on play-dates. It wouldn't be the standard script written for men, but hey—he'd thrown that out the window ages ago, along with his standard, traditional job.

When you make your living questioning conventional wisdom, it's second nature to challenge entrenched thinking. You don't buy in because you feel you have no other choice; you find a new way. Your way. Maybe that's the right attitude to bring to love and relationships, too: find a new way. Maybe the end product won't look a thing like you imagined. But maybe it will turn out to be even better.

Chapter 11

Learning to Live with the Failure

You can't sign up for the entrepreneurial life with a part-time commitment. The nature of the game is that success as an entrepreneur will take everything you have and then some. You have to be all in. Along the way, you're going to risk a whole bunch of things in order to bring your vision to life. You'll risk money, relationships, your belongings, your reputation, sometimes even your health. I've risked, compromised, and occasionally even lost all these things (and more!) at various points in my career. While the things I've had to risk have changed from year to year and project to project, there's one risk that has been ever-present, and perpetually tied up in all the others: failure.

When you take a risk, failure is always on the table. Failure can take many shapes and forms. And because the buck always stops with you, no matter what unique form your failure experience takes, it's always going to leave its mark.

On some level you probably already know that if you're not making mistakes, you're not really risking anything. Makes perfect sense, intellectually. Only, you don't want to make mistakes. The thought of making a colossal one that triggers your company's collapse isn't at all reassuring, even though you've no doubt heard that failure doesn't hold you back in the long run—it's *fear* of failure that will limit your brilliant career. Those are brave words, but having to weather failure isn't something you're in any hurry to do, even though you know that entrepreneurs consider it both a rite of passage and a badge of honour to fail at some point in their careers. But look at the facts, here. Most great entrepreneurs really did bomb at one time or another. Donald Trump declared bankruptcy twice. Colonel Sanders had his chicken recipe turned down by restaurants over a thousand times. Bill Gates's first start-up was a company called Traf-O-Data (no, I've never heard of it either).

I don't wake up every day thinking about the possibility of failure—not anymore, anyway. But the knowledge that I might fail in something I've tried is always with me. I've learned to acknowledge that fear of failure and keep moving forward with my plans. In this way, the entrepreneur is like a tightrope walker. You have to move forward with confidence and strength, even though you know that one misstep could topple you.

It's Not Us, It's You

For many entrepreneurs, the failure experience starts long before they launch their first business. Entrepreneurs are born with all sorts of innate qualities—impatience, restlessness, opportunism, for instance—that render them "essentially ungovernable" (in the words of one of Tony Lacavera's teachers) in conventional school, social, or corporate settings.

As a boy, entrepreneur Tim Moore—who built AMJ Campbell and Premiere Executive Suites into businesses that are among the largest in their categories—was so passionate about sports that he paid little heed to his studies and wound up failing three grades before he finally graduated from high school, several years behind the classmates he started with. Throughout his schooling, Tim was told repeatedly by his teachers that he "didn't have the aptitude for academics." "Those words rang in my ears for a long time," says Tim. So here was a kid who, in a setting measured by academic performance, was being told he couldn't "do" academic performance. Meanwhile, areas in which he did achieve enormous success, such as his school's basketball team (which he captained), went largely unnoticed on his report card. If that's not telling a kid he's a failure, I don't know what is. And it's a great example of how so often, until an entrepreneur achieves monetary success, the attributes that will eventually make him successful—leading others, for instance—are overlooked while his inabilities—say, to sit down and complete his homework—become the material that marks him as a failure.

This pattern often continues at work. Before Derek Bullen was the founder and CEO of S.i. Systems, a leading Calgary-based IT staffing firm, he was a failed employee. His flaw? The belief that his compensation should reflect the value he felt he'd contributed to his employer. A former software developer, Derek went back to his boss repeatedly to renegotiate his salary, a move that was triggered any time he hit some development milestone that had contributed significant value to the company he was working for.

"I was developing better and better products," he says. "I wanted to be rewarded for them." Then, one day, Derek did the single thing that "good" employees are never supposed to do—he issued an ultimatum: more money. Or else. His employer went with "or else" and fired Derek. He would be fired three times by three different companies before he finally turned a part-time programming gig into a full-time business that now does close to $300 million in annual sales.

Many entrepreneurs I know have a checkered employment history; I lost my share of jobs often because of entrepreneurial behaviour that was mistaken for insubordination. Merit Travel founder Michael Merrithew also worked his way through a succession of management consulting and marketing jobs before he finally struck out on his own. "I very quickly got bored. I couldn't seem to sink my teeth into anything, and I couldn't seem to do a specific role for more than six months before I wanted to move on," he recalls.

It's not that we enjoyed being fired or took pleasure in moving from employer to employer. By virtue of who we were as people, we simply didn't fit into a corporate setting. In that world, we were failing.

The Shame Game

The problem with the "it's not us, it's you" failure experiences is that they often happen long before an entrepreneur tastes the freedom and independence of entrepreneurship. And without that context, it's easy to look at your failure to play by the rules in school or in the workplace as a deep character flaw. I remember coming home from my early experiences at work feeling defeated and deflated. I wondered what was wrong with me and why I couldn't just fit in like my colleagues. On my worst days, I felt ashamed that I couldn't be like the other administrative assistants I worked with and simply do my job.

This shame game is dangerous, because it clouds your vision and your perception of your ability to succeed. As the renowned shame researcher Brené Brown writes in her book *Daring Greatly*, shame is essentially a feeling of innate wrongness and isolation. And when you're experiencing shame, you're actually telling yourself that there's something deeply wrong with you—not only with specific actions you've taken or words you've said, but with you— *as a person*. I can't think of any feeling more likely to douse your self-esteem, entrepreneurial spirit, or the creative drive you'll need to bring your business to reality. The work of building a business is hard enough—you can't bring it your all if you're playing hurt.

If you're currently in or have ever been in a school or work setting where, by virtue of the fact that you just don't fit in, you're labelled a failure, you've got to take immediate steps to protect yourself. Entrepreneurship isn't a sprint—it's a marathon. You have to preserve your mental energy for the long haul. So how do you do this? First, it's a good idea to acknowledge—if only to yourself—that while you may be struggling in *their* world, you'll thrive when you have the opportunity to call your own shots.

Tim Moore called on his innate rebelliousness to get him through a slew of tough years during which he was underestimated by his teachers and written off as poor student who couldn't cut it intellectually. As a teenager, when his teachers urged him to take a trade rather than go to university, he made a conscious decision to ignore them. "I told myself it was their advice, but it wasn't my advice," he says. Tim told himself that *he* would be the one to decide what he could and could not do. So, with virtually no moral support from his teachers and no financial support from his parents, he applied to university, earned a master's degree, and eventually found his footing as an entrepreneur.

Avoiding Failure

Because failure—and the shame our culture attaches to it—is so painful, your first response may be to avoid it completely. You'll get a lot of support in this department. When you're preparing to step up to the plate and swing hard, you'll attract a lot of nay-saying—some of it from other people. And while naysaying from others—be they friends, relatives, competitors, or people who comment on your company blog—can be hurtful, it's nowhere near as soul-destroying as naysaying that comes from yourself.

When I was first approached to participate in *Dragons' Den*, I was a mature adult and seasoned entrepreneur with a slew of failures under my belt—two divorces, a couple of Venture satellite offices that had to be closed early, some bad investments, and so on. I'd experienced, lived through, and learned from these failures and I knew—on an intellectual level at least—that such defeats were endurable. But the idea of being on a potentially popular television show terrified me. I was afraid of being under a microscope, I worried about how I would look and sound on television, I stressed over the degree to which the show would pull me away from my other business commitments. I was intrigued by the opportunity, but I was also terrified that I would step into the limelight and fail.

In creative circles, this negative internal fear is called *resistance*. In his work *The War of Art*—which is as much about entrepreneurial ventures as artistic endeavours—author Steven Pressfield describes resistance as an innate negative response that is triggered whenever we begin to reach for something that we truly want—especially when the thing we're reaching for lies beyond our comfort zone. Resistance shows up in different ways, but usually as some sort of excuse to avoid the risks associated with stepping up your game—the urgent need to check your email when you should be drafting a business plan for your new satellite office or, in my case, focusing on all the things that could go wrong if I went on television and failed.

The best way to arm yourself against resistance is to recognize it when it strikes and dismiss is as quickly as you can. This is not to say that internal misgivings are useless. On the contrary, gut checks are essential. All along my gut told me that agreeing to appear on *Dragons' Den* was an opportunity that would change my life in amazing and unexpected ways. My fears—about whether I would look dumb, or that the show would be a flop—got me in my throat. It's like they literally wanted to spare me from the humiliation of failing on TV by choking off my dream before it had a chance to take root. I wallowed in the fear for a little while. But then I carefully assessed the pros and cons, pushed through my fear, and went with my gut. I'm so glad I did, because many extraordinary opportunities have presented themselves thanks to my work on TV—this book is just one example. Sometimes I can't believe I might have forsaken them because I was afraid to fail.

Seeing Failure as Part of Your Training

The inventor and entrepreneur Thomas Edison famously said that "the fastest way to succeed is to double your failure rate." I couldn't agree more. Every successful entrepreneur I know has experienced her share of failures: near bankruptcies, product recalls, inability to secure adequate financing, or just a good old-fashioned lack of customers. It's not the mistakes themselves that help to hone your entrepreneurial skill—rather, it's what you learn from your mistakes, and the degree to which you're willing to grow from them.

John Risley credits his willingness to learn from a big mistake he made in the early days of Clearwater Seafoods in helping him build the company into one of the world's largest seafood companies.

It was the late 1970s, and he and Clearwater co-founder Colin MacDonald were exhausted and at their breaking point. They hadn't taken a day off in three years and slept at work a couple of nights a week. "It would have been impossible to work any harder than we worked," he says. And while they were making a living, their earnings were nowhere near "commensurate with the effort."

"I thought to myself, *There has to be a better way, this is crazy. I'm not going to become a millionaire doing what I'm doing now. I've got to think about my business differently,*" he recalls.

John sensed his mistake had to do with Clearwater's business model. He and his partner were working as hard as physically possible, paying close attention to expenses, and pricing their seafood competitively. There simply wasn't room to wrangle more profits from the existing business. But with no formal business training, John lacked the technical skills to figure out how to improve the company. So he made a decision that would alter his company's trajectory—he enrolled in a part-time management for small business program at Harvard. Over the next few years, he completed a series of three-week sessions that taught him some fundamental business concepts, including the one that would transform his company into one of the largest seafood players in the world: competitive advantage.

"I learned that without a competitive advantage, our margins were simply a function of the hard work we were putting into the business," he says. So he came home and spent the next few years figuring out how to introduce a competitive advantage into the business. He started with technological improvements to keep the lobster fresher longer, then purchased fishing licences and associated quota. These changes allowed the company to control its supply chain, resulting in higher margins for the company.

John's mistake—starting with a business model unlikely to yield strong profits—led him to learn new skills and create a system that was wildly successful. Throughout his career, John says, mistakes have made him "a better entrepreneur." Improvement, he explains, "is honed with losses, it's not honed with profits." I couldn't agree more. Profits spur you to do more of the same thing; losses and mistakes push you to do things better.

Getting Comfortable with the Teacher

It's one thing to know that failure can teach you a lot. But if you don't train yourself to get comfortable with the teacher, you'll never be able to the face the lessons embedded in your failings. Spanx founder Sara Blakely, a.k.a. the youngest female self-made billionaire in history, tells a wonderful story about how she learned to become comfortable with failure. When she was growing up, her dad, a lawyer, would ask each of his kids what they'd failed at that day. If no one had any failures to report, he was disappointed. What Sara took from this was that failure isn't cause for shame. It was evidence that she was trying new things and taking risks. Her father clearly prized risk-taking, so if she wanted to please him, she had to stretch beyond her comfort zone. By the law of averages, sometimes she was going to stretch and fall flat on her face.

This lesson stayed with her throughout her career. Before launching Spanx, she worked for a Florida office-supply company, where her job was to sell fax machines. Door-to-door. As she gave her spiel, some people ripped up her business card right in front of her. But along the way, she says, she mastered the art of the cold call, which came in handy when she was trying to find a hosiery company to mass produce her Spanx prototype. She was repeatedly told "no" then, too, until she received a call from the manager of a North Carolina factory who'd turned her down two weeks earlier. His daughters, he told her, had insisted that he manufacture Blakely's product.

You don't just need faith in yourself and your creation to develop the kind of invisible shield that protects you from taking rejection personally or taking your own mistakes to heart. You also have to develop an almost forensic ability to view your missteps and outright failures objectively. *Maybe my idea wasn't as great as I thought. Maybe it just doesn't work for that particular investor. Or maybe my pitch wasn't persuasive. Maybe I should take some of the feedback I got and rethink how I approach the market.* If you can remove your emotions from the equation, you'll see more clearly that other variables are at play—and your mistakes will become opportunities for learning, not self-punishment. It's the best way to recover and move on quickly.

Michael Merrithew developed this forensic ability when he was still in the throes of the "it's not us, it's you" failure stage. During the decade or so he spent moving from one job to the next, he became increasingly frustrated with the limitations of his jobs and also, in some cases, with himself because of his seeming inability to settle down. But rather than take his "inability to keep a job" as proof that he was somehow an unworthy person, he began analyzing his experiences carefully to determine what, specifically, was frustrating him.

The problem wasn't that he didn't enjoy his work, nor was it that he wanted to be on vacation versus showing up at the office each day. Rather, Michael's frustration was that once he felt he'd learned the basic ropes of his job—which generally took him about six months—he immediately began looking for ways to enrich it, either by making the work more challenging or by taking it in a new direction. And while he sometimes was able to innovate on the job, his desire to make changes or improvements was never fully sated. "I finally realized that I had to do my own thing," he says. But rather than leap at the first possible opportunity, Michael took his time, waiting for the right opportunity to reveal itself while he continued to work at increasingly senior marketing and management roles, building his business toolkit the entire time.

"I went into my jobs knowing I was going to give my employer 110 percent," he says. "I reminded myself I was gaining experience I wouldn't otherwise get." He took advantage of any training, coaching, or mentoring opportunities the companies he worked for offered, and also paid close attention to how his employers handled everything from budgeting to research to business processes. "It was like I was getting paid to go to school," he says. In short, by the time he was ready to take over and grow his own travel agency, the one-time "terrible employee" graduated from a failed corporate career with a custom-made MBA that he would use to help build the largest specialty travel company in Canada.

Why "This Might Not Work" Should Be Music to Your Ears

When it came to growing his building supplies company, Vancouver entrepreneur John Gross employed two strategies that the conventional wisdom of the day told him would spell disaster for his company.

For starters, he decided to source and manufacture his building supplies in China. And while China was well known for cost-effective production, in 1998, when John founded Peak Products, the nation was not considered a high-quality producer of building supplies. Friends and colleagues told him he was crazy for taking a risk on Chinese manufacturing, and that he needed to guard against poor-quality products.

A few years later, John signed a deal to become an exclusive supplier to Home Depot, a move that sparked numerous warnings from those same well-wishers that "putting all his eggs in one basket" was a risky move.

John knew the reason these two strategies were frowned on was because they presented clear and present dangers to his business. But his gut told him he was developing a rock-solid business plan. His instincts proved correct: the business has experienced considerable growth and stability thanks to his ability to compete with high-quality, low-cost suppliers. And while his competitors have to manage relationships with multiple retailers, he has to work with only one. What's more, his move to China was prescient. When he started, he was the only Canadian supplier he knew of sourcing products from China. Today, thousands of companies worldwide follow in his footsteps.

"It's absolutely critical that you challenge the status quo. That's where the breakthroughs and paradigm shifts come from," he says. "You tell yourself, *I'm not going to accept the conventional wisdom; I'm going to take a different approach*. It's how you, as an entrepreneur, differentiate yourself from everyone else out there."

Test Runs

When I first started trying to expand Venture Communications beyond its Calgary office, I took an aggressive approach, opening in short order a slew of offices in Halifax, Ottawa, Edmonton, and Winnipeg. But I underestimated just how much time and effort I would personally have to invest to make each satellite office a stand-alone success. Within a few years, I was forced to close down more than half the satellite offices I'd opened. This was one of my first big failure experiences in business, and it taught me two important lessons.

First, I learned that failure isn't as bad as it might appear. When I opened the offices, I badly wanted them to be a success. But when problems started to reveal themselves—a failure to replicate the strong corporate culture we had in the Calgary office, the challenges of building a client base in a new market—I started to worry about what would happen if these offices failed. Would my reputation as a businesswoman be forever tarnished? Would I sustain a huge financial hit? It turned out that those failed satellite offices closed not with a bang but a whimper—our employees found new opportunities, our leases expired, and we just left. Failure wasn't nearly as big a deal as I thought it would be.

The second lesson I learned is that failure is rarely final. Just like the old sales adage tells us that the first "no" usually means "not yet," I've learned that failure should often be interpreted as "not yet" or "not quite like this."

I took the lessons from my failed satellites and used them to help me figure out how to grow the company outside Calgary. I knew that opening a second office would take more time, energy, and commitment than I had originally thought. So rather than spread my efforts across the country, I focused on a single new market. Today, Venture has two very successful Canadian offices, in Calgary and Toronto. Would the Toronto office have been as successful were it not for my Round One failures in other Canadian cities? Probably not—because my early taste of defeat made me not only wiser but hungrier for success, too.

Tanya Shaw first envisioned her now hugely successful Me-Ality body scanner and size-matching station in 1994, almost two decades before it went to market. Then a young entrepreneur better known as a custom-fit pattern creator, Tanya pitched her business concept to a panel of business experts with the ultimate hope of scoring either investment or a mentor, or both. Their response: "Whoa, whoa, whoa. You're way ahead of what the market is ready for." The experts told Tanya her idea would fail if she tried to bring it to market then, and that she needed to scale her vision down and look at, say, automating the creation of custom-clothing patterns as a way to build credibility within the world of custom-fit fashion.

Was Tanya disappointed at having to change course? Would it have been easy to leave that 1994 panel presentation feeling as though her big idea was doomed to fail? Absolutely. But she was also able to see the wisdom of what the experts were telling her. "I started out with such a big vision, and their advice helped me take a step in the right direction. I was still focused on the vision, but taking smaller steps toward it," she says. After the presentation, Tanya honed in on the home-sewing market and developed pattern-customization software, which she licensed to pattern-creation giants Butterick, Vogue, and McCall's two years later.

Try, Try Again

It can be helpful to look at your failure as a prototype that you need to discard in order to find the winning model. Toronto entrepreneur Jeff Anders took his online media business *The Mark* through numerous iterations before he finally found a business model that was sustainable. After working first as a management consultant and next as a volunteer on then Liberal leader Michael Ignatieff's election campaign, Jeff decided to launch a *Huffington Post*-style online news and opinion site for Canadian expatriates. He scored a partner—a seasoned newspaper executive—and spent a year raising capital to get his idea off the ground. That's where he got his first taste of failure. It seems 2009 was "probably the worst time to try and raise capital"—especially for a media company, given the turmoil of the news industry at the time. Jeff encountered more no's than he'd ever met in his life, and some proved hugely painful. He cancelled attending his best friend's bachelor party in Europe so he could attend a meeting with an investor—who called shortly before the meeting to cancel.

"I got knocked down, then I got back up time and time again," he remembers. But the constant refusals helped him work on his pitch and his strategy. During his failed meetings, he noticed many investors asking who else was in on the investment—but Jeff was never able to provide a name. Then he convinced an on-the-fence investor—who was willing to put up 20 percent if others came on board, too—to allow Jeff to use his name in order to score additional investment. If Jeff wasn't successful in attracting enough money, he simply wouldn't hold his anchor investor—or any others whose money was contingent on the anchor investor—to their commitments. The strategy worked, and after 18 months Jeff had enough money to launch *The Mark*.

But he soon realized that he needed a more robust business model if the company was going to be financially viable. His business model went through a series of iterations. Knowing that he had access to excellent content and celebrity and other well-known writers, he launched a customized content service for conferences, which included well-researched features on conference topics and in-depth interviews with speakers. The idea was interesting, but he soon learned there were too few conferences with a large enough budget to make it viable. Next, he tried selling *The Mark*'s content to other media outlets—again, a decent idea in theory, but when tested, proved to be a no-go. For the next few years, he kept reworking his business model. Meanwhile, his funding was running low, and at one point a major news outlet, recognizing the high-level content his company was producing, hired away the bulk of Jeff's staff.

The repeated failures were a harrowing experience, Jeff says. "If I wasn't so absolutely certain that this was the path for me to create something lasting and meaningful, then I would probably have given up," he adds. But when he encountered naysayers, obstacles, or people who told him his ideas wouldn't work, he asked himself a question similar to what a young Tim Moore asked himself: "Are they right or am I right? And every time, I reached the conclusion that I was right and it just strengthened my resolve," he says.

Today, Jeff has built a successful business model that sees his company continuing to run the news site. It also produces highly customized online content, offers webinars for blue-chip companies, and distributes opinion pieces by high-level dignitaries to global media outlets. And all those failures, or iterations, have helped push the company to be unique and truly innovative, which in turn sets him apart from his competition.

Know When to Throw Away Your Safety Net

So you know that failure is inevitable, and also that it can be help-ful. You expect it, you know it might not be as brutal as you fear, and you're prepared to change course if your plans don't survive in the real world. Now you need to recommit to your business and burn the bridges that connect you to the safe, comfortable world. That's because your business will take everything you have, and the lull of security could derail your efforts to feel the fear of failure and do it anyway.

When Cactus Clubs Cafe founder Richard Jaffray quit uni-versity and moved to Vancouver to start a restaurant, he told all his family and friends about his big dreams. Everyone he knew was aware that the aspiring entrepreneur was forgoing the secure life of employment as an engineer for the far riskier one of the entrepreneur. Looking back, he sees that he backed himself into a corner where, in order to save face, he had to make a go of it.

"Everyone knew what I was up to," he says. "I felt I had no choice but to be successful." You've heard the stories of the extra-ordinary lengths people can go to when their backs are against the wall. For entrepreneurs, dealing with failure is a process of welcoming it and fighting it with everything we have at the same time. I've learned more about myself from my failures and near misses than I have from success.

* * *

The most important reason you need to make peace with fail-ure is that the fear of it—and the reality of it—never leave you. "I'm still terrified to fail," says entrepreneur John Risley, after four decades of entrepreneurship. "It's what drives me." And while I understand the importance of failure for entrepreneurs, I get what he's saying. Being afraid to fail is a natural, human emotion. And in my experience, the higher you rise, the scarier it is to fall. On one level, I know from experience that failure isn't as big a deal as I often make it out to be. On another, the better known I become, the more pressure I feel to avoid failure.

But feeling and doing are two different things. Though I feel pressure to succeed, I've trained myself to follow my instincts and let go of what other people think. I know that failure is always on the table, so I feel the fear and I do what I need to do anyway. If you want to make your vision a reality, you'll need to learn to do the same.

Chapter 12

Success: The Good, the Bad, and the Ugly

Success is sweet. I'm not talking about just the material rewards, although they are very pleasant. Even more gratifying is the freedom you have to write the next chapters of your life—and the sense of pride you take in having come this far. It's a feel-good story: you hung in there, built something of value, and realized your dream.

But real life isn't a novel, and getting what you've always wished for isn't a happy ending. It's just another kind of beginning. Now, many entrepreneurs do feel a particular sense of wonder and satisfaction when a longed-for symbol of success is finally achieved. Greg Chamandy, for instance, told me that he'd always dreamed of one day ringing the bell on the New York Stock Exchange. When Gildan Activewear went through an IPO in 1998 and that dream finally came true, it was one of the proudest moments of his professional life. At the ceremony, he was presented with a beautiful miniature bronze replica of the famous bull and bear statue that stands at the entrance to the Stock Exchange, and later he was interviewed on CNN. For an entrepreneur who started out in the shipping room of his grandfather's Montreal garment factory, it was quite a day.

But in the end, it was just a day. His life wasn't altered beyond recognition. The next morning he woke up and it was business as usual. The euphoria didn't last all that long. He was still the same person he'd always been, multi-tasking like crazy, only now he had that cool new bronze memento in his office.

From the outside, success can seem like the promised land. It sure did to me. I had to get there to find out that though the trappings can be dazzling, they come at a cost—one that you haven't, in fact, already paid. You've paid only your dues, professionally and personally. Now there's something new: an emotional price tag attached to success itself. And every entrepreneur, in one way or another, is forced to pay up.

Be Careful What You Wish For

Success doesn't always involve a lot of money. Just ask a restaurateur, or a clothing designer, or any entrepreneur who's founded a top-ranked company in an industry with a low profit margin. In many cases, success is really more about recognition than anything else.

But in one way, recognition is like money: it can change everything. It can make you feel more secure and more willing to take risks, or it can go to your head. It can be wonderfully liberating and broadening, or painfully distancing and isolating. It can inspire great admiration, or elicit tremendous jealousy. It can affect how you treat others and how others treat you. You may become a more expansive, giving human being, or you may turn into an arrogant jerk. How well you become known outside your own field can have a significant influence. If success thrusts you into the public eye, even for just 15 minutes, you may not always attract the kind of attention you want.

Don't get me wrong. I don't have mixed feelings about success. I'm not interested in trading my own. But there's a lot I wish I'd known and hadn't had to learn the hard way, starting with the fact that recognition has a tipping point, and once you pass it, it can start to feel more like a constricting and limiting force than a pat on the back that encourages you to keep going. Before *Dragons' Den*, I wasn't known outside the marketing community, but I had recognition within it. Venture won industry awards and made those best-managed company lists; I was asked to give speeches and to serve on committees and boards and so forth. All this made me feel more confident that I was doing a good job, and that confidence propelled me forward.

After I started appearing on the show, I got even more recognition, but it was a different kind. People occasionally recognized me on the street, which was strange at first and, to be honest, I've never really got used to it. The thing is, I'm not recognized for the core skills that I've built over the past quarter-century as a marketer and businesswoman. I'm recognized for being on TV and for having enough money to fund start-ups that I believe in.

And again, I'm totally not complaining. Most of the attention I get is wonderfully warm, and it feels incredibly good to be liked. A small degree of fame has also opened doors to encounters with interesting people from all walks of life, people I probably would never have met otherwise. And in many cases, the people I've met have not only inspired me personally but also helped me work through tricky problems in my business. Entrepreneurs rely heavily on our professional networks because we simply don't have all the answers we need to confront the challenges we encounter daily. A few months ago, I was trying to figure out whether a strategic decision I was making at YouInc was the right move. Because of the new network of experts I have thanks to *Dragons' Den*, I had the phone number of a hugely successful tech-entrepreneur in my back pocket. I called him, we met for coffee, and he helped me work through the problem. That's a huge side benefit of media exposure: you meet fascinating people and you're exposed to so many new perspectives. It's broadening, in many ways.

And yet, it's also been narrowing, because I've become more wary of other people and less trusting. One reason, frankly, is that I get hit up for money almost daily. Charities approach me regularly, of course, which is understandable. And just as I always have, I donate time and money to the causes that I care about passionately, like making sure kids across Canada have breakfast every day, regardless of where they live or how much money their parents have; and serving as an honorary captain of the Royal Canadian Navy, visiting troops overseas to support their efforts on our nation's behalf.

What is less understandable is the barrage of emails, texts, and voicemails from people who seem to think that, if they tell me their troubles, I'll write them a cheque on the spot. I've heard it all: *I'm going to school. I need a car. I need your help because I can't get ahead.* I also receive marriage proposals, some of which are so romantic I find them hard to resist, like the one from the guy who wrote, "Marry me because you're rich." Many of the strangers who ask me for money seem to think I owe it to them because I was poor once, too—I know how bad it feels and should put them out of their misery with a cash transfusion. They seem to view me as a fairy godmother or an ATM, rather than as a human being.

Now, I am not some wildly famous celebrity. We're not talking Kim Kardashian here. Yet even my minor brush with fame, Canadian-style, has made me a bit more suspicious of people's motives than I used to be. Sometimes midway through a business meeting I've realized that this is not the serious session I thought it was. These people wanted to meet someone from a TV show. This has happened enough times that I've learned to be more careful about agreeing to meetings, and a little more cynical, which is a bit sad, actually. But success is a package deal. You don't get to cherry-pick the parts you like and chuck the rest.

I'm a pleaser. I want to be liked and approved of, and success has in some ways made that quite a bit more difficult. I often feel I'm letting people down, not because I'm doing anything wrong but because their expectations can be so unrealistic. It's hard to say "no" even when the request is not reasonable, and I have to say "no" a *lot* more than I did when I was struggling and had a hard time getting my calls returned. I think this is one reason many successful people buffer themselves with gatekeepers and layers of assistants: it's not that they feel they're better than other people— it's that other people sometimes unintentionally make them feel so bad about themselves.

My friend Jann Arden has a telling story to illustrate what I'm talking about. Now, Jann is as beloved for her charm, humour, and engagingly down-home candour as she is for her music, which is really saying something. But for her, that means all the world's a stage—whether she wants to perform or not. Everyone expects her to behave in a certain way, even when she's just rushed her mother to the emergency room. Picture this: Jann, terrified her mother was dying, was standing beside her gurney in the hospital. Doctors had just used paddles to shock her mother's heart. Jann was distraught. And then she heard a woman say, "Oh my God, Jann Arden's here!" The woman began rummaging around in her purse for a pen. Jann remembers, "I had this feeling of anger and hatred coming up through my esophagus. I could have killed her with a glance." The fan didn't see her as a woman in the midst of a life-or-death crisis; she just saw Jann Arden, The Singer.

The story has a great coda, though. As Jann tells it, just as her surge of rage was cresting and she'd repelled the woman, her mom's "bony little hand" reached out and grabbed hers. Then Jann heard her mom say, "Would it kill you to sign that piece of paper?" She reminded her daughter that being available to fans was just part of her job description. (Jann's mom recovered, I'm happy to report.)

Obviously, someone who is recognizably famous is going to deal with more intrusive forms of interest. But in one form or another, most successful entrepreneurs have to deal with what Jann describes. You're seen as less human, somehow, for having made it. Some people will behave as though the normal rules of interaction no longer apply. An acquaintance you barely know will be offended if you don't help his nephew get a summer job; at a cocktail party, you'll be buttonholed by people demanding help of some sort. These ramped-up external demands exact an emotional toll. It's difficult, and probably inadvisable, not to become more guarded and closed off as a result. This isn't such a huge problem if you've always viewed yourself as a savvy, street-wise type. But if your self-image is that you're an open-to-the-universe person with a generous spirit—well, it's a blow. It's a loss of innocence, and that's not a minor loss. You've learned that some people are just out to use you, and while that may be a necessary fact to recognize and accept, it doesn't feel good to know that the pool of people you can trust has shrunk.

There's a related phenomenon, too. Fewer people will tell you the truth anymore, even though you now need to hear it more than ever. Think back to when you were just starting out and had this crazy idea for a business—you'd tell others your plans, and the naysayers would begin to bleat their misgivings. Often they didn't understand your idea or what motivated you to pursue it. Or they called you crazy for taking a risk that actually terrified them. (Sometimes, too, they raised legitimate points that you knew you'd be wise to address as you honed your business plan.)

Now, fast-forward. You've finally proven the skeptics wrong—you're running a successful business. But whereas before you couldn't get anyone to agree with you, now you can't get anybody to level with you or disagree with your take on something. You're the boss, so they tell you what they think you want to hear. People don't want to tick you off or get on your bad side, or they figure you must know best because you're running the place. The naysayers have turned into yeahsayers—and that isn't good for your business, your ego, or your perception of reality.

Perspective. Perspective. Perspective.

For a morality tale about the perils of success, it's hard to do better than *Citizen Kane*. The protagonist begins his career idealistically, seeking social justice, but success warps him. He becomes a ruthless power-seeker—and a thoroughly miserable person. Sure, it's a movie. But the story is based on the life of William Randolph

Hearst, the publishing magnate, and an entrepreneur if ever there was one.

Steve Jobs told his biographer, Walter Isaacson, about watching people who struck it rich at Apple rushing out to buy Rolls-Royces and huge houses that they felt compelled to hire house managers to run. Then they hired managers to manage their house managers. Then their wives got plastic surgery "and turned into these bizarre people. This was not how I wanted to live. It's crazy," Jobs decided. So he made a promise to himself. He told himself: "I'm not going to let this money ruin my life."

Think about that for a minute. Here's a guy who'd achieved success beyond his—beyond anyone's—wildest dreams. His number one concern? That if he wasn't careful, success would wreck his life. In her eulogy for Jobs, his sister, Mona Simpson, says he worked hard to raise kids who were grounded and to have a house that felt like a home rather than an intimidating palace. She mentioned that he picked her up at the airport himself when she came to visit, rather than sending a limo. "This is not to say that he didn't enjoy his success. He enjoyed it a lot, just minus a few zeros," is how Simpson, an acclaimed novelist, put it.

Remembering where you come from is vitally important to offsetting the head-swelling, lifestyle-distorting aspects of success. But how do you stay true to yourself when you feel like a kid in a candy shop? It requires vigilance, or you'll find yourself cramming all the candy you can into your mouth and then, eventually, crashing after a massive sugar high. Candy tastes great, but those are empty calories and they're not exactly good for your health or your sense of well-being. When you binge on the stuff that comes along with success, whether it's money or admiration or power, you can wind up feeling bloated, yet somehow empty.

Now, I'm not suggesting you run yourself ragged starting a business and then, once it's a bona fide hit, pursue a monastic lifestyle. It would be pretty pointless to work so hard for success, then not enjoy it. I certainly enjoy mine, and I've been known to buy shoes that I don't strictly need and to go a little crazy in the toy store when one of my grandkids is with me. But I have my family, my friends, and my philanthropic passions to help me keep things in perspective and to give my life a sense of purpose—beyond the passion and purpose that my work already brings to my life.

Christine Magee, the co-founder and president of Sleep Country, attributes her ability to stay grounded, real, and humble in part to her family and friends, who remain unimpressed with her even as they cheer her on. She also credits her husband, Al Magee, whom she calls her best friend, confidant, and most enthusiastic cheerleader. Al, now retired, was Sleep Country's first sales manager and subsequently the president and CEO of Magee TV. Christine says, "He has built me up and supported every move, every decision. And he is also honest, so he tells me the truth even when I don't want to hear it. That's perspective."

Blue Ant Media company founder Michael MacMillan met his wife, lawyer Cathy Spoel, at university, so she's been along for the ride since the earliest days of Atlantis Films. Michael once told me that while Cathy has been highly supportive, what's really helped him keep his feet on the ground through that amazing ride is the fact that she couldn't care less about his media empire. She's been known to ask, "What are the names of those channels that you own? What are they called again?"

You need to surround yourself with people like that in order to stay grounded. When you're a major player and you keep coming out on top, the danger is that you'll start believing your own press and come down with a severe case of hubris. You need people in your life who believe in you unreservedly, yet don't buy the hype—people who can act as a balancing force, like Cathy Spoel and Al Magee. I don't know of a single entrepreneur who makes it through success with his or her character unscathed unless there's *someone* in their lives to act as a leavening force. Usually, it's a spouse, family member, friend, or colleague, but who knows? Maybe your auto mechanic will weigh in with sage advice. The point is that you'll need to keep a sense of perspective or you run the risk of becoming a thoroughly insufferable egotist.

You'll *really* need to stay grounded if success taps you on the shoulder early, as it did in Michael MacMillan's case. He was just 27 years old when, in 1984, he and his partners at Atlantis Films won an Oscar for *Boys and Girls*, a film based on an Alice Munro story and starring the then unknown Megan Follows. The Oscar catapulted Atlantis Films into the big time. "It blew open doors in Hollywood that would have taken maybe forever or certainly another decade" to open, Michael says. If he'd been star-struck or surrounded by people who were, he would have been toast. Fortunately, he realized early on that allowing himself to get caught up in "all the . . . accolades and showbiz and Hollywood stuff" would lead to trouble. (One of the troubles it can lead to, by the way, is provoking envy and bitterness among friends, family members, and colleagues.) Michael grasped early the necessity of preserving a "regular part of your life."

Entrepreneurs find different ways to maintain perspective. Christine Magee told me she distinctly remembers when her daughters were little and she'd come in the door after crazy-busy and often frustrating days. Her daughters would "run up and throw themselves into [her] arms with such abandon and love me regardless of what I accomplished that day . . . or not . . . or did well or didn't. It was in those moments that I quickly remembered what is important. . . . Sure, I need to be good if not great at work, but at the end of the day all of that was unimportant compared to the love, safety, and development of my girls."

In a funny way, my insecurities help me stay grounded. A few months ago, I was invited to speak at a luncheon for business-women in Toronto. I had a good idea of what I wanted to say, but I didn't bring any notes because I find I speak better when it's straight from the heart. I arrived after most of the attendees were already seated. When I walked into the cavernous confer-ence room and saw all those women waiting to hear me, my entire speech flew right out of my head. I just couldn't believe so many people would pay to hear what I had to say. I made my way to the stage and, with a wildly beating heart, launched into my talk. It wasn't just stage fright that got me through. I had an overwhelm ing sense of gratitude that I was able to share what I know with so many people, plus a feeling of humility that so many people took time out of their day to listen to what I had to say. I hold on to my nerves and insecurity because they keep me grounded, real, and grateful for what I have.

Walking on the Dark Side

Jann Arden is hardly the first artist to deal with the loneliness of life on the road by drinking too much. The pressures of success can lead many successful entrepreneurs down the same dark path. As I mentioned earlier, entrepreneurs, like artists, fervently embrace independence and risk, and are fundamentally creative beings who express themselves through business rather than music or painting or poetry. Yes, we articulate our ideas in a commercial forum, but the driving force is the same: the need for creative self-expression. I like to say that we pursue art for commerce's sake. Like artists, we are non-conformists who live by our wits and by tapping into our intuition and emotions. We pursue our dreams relentlessly: we're willing to live in a garret, if necessary, to make them come true.

Artists from Vincent Van Gogh to Keith Richards tend to be romanticized for their self-destructive behaviour. Fortunately entrepreneurs don't tend to run around lopping off their own ears, as Van Gogh did. But when it comes to stormy moods, substance abuse, and the like, some of them are right up there with the most notorious writers, artists, and rock stars. Yet this behaviour is often considered a big surprise, because people don't understand that the motives are essentially the same for entrepreneurs as they are for artists. Both feel they have their souls on the line; both may find success leads to excess, or that success induces massive insecurity.

It's because I know entrepreneurs who have struggled mightily with the toxic underbelly of success that I was interested in the work of Dr. Marsha Vannicelli, a clinical associate professor of psychology at Harvard Medical School and the former director of the Substance Abuse Outpatient Clinic at Boston's renowned McLean Hospital. Dr. Vannicelli also has a private practice in Cambridge, Massachusetts, where she counsels CEOs and other stressed-out executives who need help managing what she describes on her website as "the downside of success."

What are some of those potential downsides? Dr. Vannicelli lists depression, anxiety, loneliness, "a sense of meaninglessness," alcohol abuse, and other "self-defeating behaviours that could jeopardize close relationships." She explains that just when stressed-out titans of business most need someone to listen and help them restore a sense of perspective, they may find themselves completely isolated. Meanwhile, their drive to succeed conflicts with their ability to invest in fulfilling relationships. It's the classic Catch-22. Add anxieties about staying ahead of the pack (which could tap into underlying fears of failure and uneasy guilt about having "too much"), and you have a combustible mix.

Sure, you may own a private island, but if you're wracked with guilt about being able to afford it, have no one to share it with, and are drinking yourself to death on the beach, what's the point?

Beast of Burden

Another emotional burden that comes with success is the responsibility for other people's money. You'll feel that weight from the start if you have investors, of course. But once you succeed, a lot more dollars are at stake, and the burden can start to feel a lot heavier.

People who may have initially invested in your company viewing it as a gamble, or viewing you as a charity case, are now looking to you with great expectations. They're counting on you to build their nest egg. If your company runs into trouble of any sort, they are not going to sit by quietly. You will be dealing with their anxiety and upset as well as your own—and worse, you will feel that you let them down.

When Yung Wu knew that his company was in serious trouble and had to restructure, he flew around to break the news, personally, to every single investor. One of them was his dad. Having to tell his father where things stood was one of the most difficult moments in his life. "If you're betting with your own dollars, it's completely acceptable to do whatever you do," he explains. "But the first dime you take from the outside, you're now a custodian of someone else's money. . . ." Once you're bartering with another person's assets, everything changes. In some ways, it can be positive: you're less tempted to take stupid risks. But in other ways, it can be negative: you never feel free of that psychic weight, and it can become too much to carry.

Yung Wu related to the story of an entrepreneur he knows who achieved stratospheric success but nevertheless felt like he was "sprinting through a minefield balancing several cartons of eggs. At some point, the eggs he was carrying were owned by other people, and he needed that off his shoulders." The entrepreneur decided to sell his company. It's one thing to leverage your own credit cards and live in a basement apartment while you're getting your business off the ground. It's another thing to feel you're risking other people's life savings. At some point, that may feel like too heavy a burden to bear.

Give and Take, Take, Take

One of the ways you know you've made it as an entrepreneur is when other people start seeing you as a meal ticket or a means to an end. I'm not just talking about random strangers. Often family members, friends, and casual acquaintances also want to trade on your connections or avail themselves of your time and expertise for free. Because we are frequently so grateful for our good fortune, entrepreneurs don't talk about the way in which success can open the door to people who want to take advantage of what has taken you years to build.

There's a famous and possibly apocryphal story about Picasso sitting in a Paris café one day when a fan approached and asked if he'd draw a quick sketch for him on a paper napkin. The story goes that Picasso graciously complied and handed over the drawing, but not before asking for a sizable sum in return. The admirer was shocked. He asked, "How can you ask for so much? It took you only a minute to draw this." "No," replied Picasso. "It took me 40 years."

I can be the most generous person in the world—until I think that someone is taking advantage of me, in which case, I shut down. I batten down the hatches even though I know that closing myself off from others will only reinforce my insecurities about whether people like the real me, or just what I can do for them.

Success can strain friendships, and sometimes you try to reduce the strain by sharing what you have. But that can backfire, big time. I know of one high-profile entrepreneur who helped bail out a friend's business. The enterprise was failing, but the entrepreneur saw its potential, believed he was making a sound investment, and thought he could help turn the company around. But because the person who was running the business was someone he trusted, a true-blue friend, he didn't do his proper due diligence. He threw money at the problem without keeping a close eye on where it was going, and one day he discovered he was being cheated. He felt his friend had preyed on his compassionate nature and his trust in him.

A costly court battle ensued and he won a judgment, but he's still trying to collect. The experience was devastating. Far worse than the financial losses or stress of the lawsuit was the betrayal by someone he thought was his friend.

Success can also put tremendous strain on your relationship with your significant other, as I talked about in Chapter 9 and Chapter 10. The truth is, you simply will not have as much time for your partner during a launch or a period of tremendous growth.

The Friend Problem

The entrepreneurial lifestyle is also hell on friendships. I've found it to be particularly hard on friendships with people who aren't entrepreneurs. The demands on my time are really different, and friends may view it as a slight if I can't get together with them or if I have to cancel at the last minute. Or they think that if I don't call for a few months, it's because I don't care. I wind up feeling frustrated because they don't understand how different my life is from theirs, and guilty because I've hurt and angered them.

Sometimes, it's as though we're speaking different languages. For instance, I say, "I'm sorry, I can't make it," and they hear, "She's unwilling to make time for me." In a way, they're right, but they don't understand the reasons. It's not because I don't value the friendship but because I have a crisis in the office that no one else can handle. Also, I *own* that office. I need the crisis to go away.

Once, I was horrified to learn that a friend of mine had gone through a serious health crisis that I heard about only many months later. I felt sick when I found out about it. What kind of person doesn't know about her friend's health crisis? And yet, I didn't.

Entrepreneurs have less time and less ability to invest in friendships, and casual friendships may simply wither and die because you can't tend to them. The people you might have enjoyed having dinner with twice a year, you're now seeing once a year for a rushed coffee—and while you're drinking it, you're wondering why you didn't use this little slice of time to see the best friend you've been neglecting. When emotional resources are limited, you have to divide them differently and accept that you simply don't have time for certain people and certain types of friendships. The issue isn't that you don't like them anymore. The issue is simply that there are people who are much more important to you, and you have to be more strategic about how you spend your time now that there's less of it. It sounds harsh, and you're likely to feel bad about it, but it's a reality of the entrepreneurial lifestyle. For the truly important people in your life, though, I encourage all entrepreneurs to find the time.

Even if you don't feel bad about it, trust that others will try to make you feel bad, especially if you're female. As a woman, I find that we're always being or feeling judged if we're not constantly in nurturing mode. Despite the many gains women have made, we still have to wear a scarlet *E* if our work takes precedence over nurturing.

Recently, I was talking to one of my dearest friends about all this. Margot Micallef is also an entrepreneur and, like me, doesn't have many deep friendships. We both know a lot of people, and neither of us doubts that the church would be fairly full if we suddenly shuffled off this mortal coil. But there would be only a handful of people in attendance who *really* knew us. Part of the reason, I think, is that we expend so much emotional energy nurturing our families that, when we add business to the mix, we have very little emotional capital left to invest in our friendships. Gender inequality doesn't help. In my line of work, I deal with many more men than women, and it's hard to develop friendships that don't look inappropriate, even when they're wholly innocent.

* * *

Success is complicated, far more so than it appears to be before you achieve it. I know, I know—you're thinking, *I like complications! The more the better!* I hear you—and I want you to handle these complications beautifully. Nothing would please me more than to see the ranks of successful entrepreneurs in this country swell exponentially, because I believe our economic future depends on it.

Conclusion

Entrepreneurs come in all shapes and sizes, but one key thing we share is our bone-deep need to strike out on our own. Other people might see our willingness to leap without a safety net as evidence of our risk-loving natures. I have no doubt that entrepreneurs are more risk tolerant than your average person. But the reality is that risk tolerance is a coping mechanism we have to develop in order to live the lives we were born to lead. Because when it comes to responding to the entrepreneurial calling, most of us feel we have no choice. Entrepreneurship isn't a job; it's an identity, a way of life, and a powerful guiding instinct.

My friend Lisa Gabriele worked in the TV industry for 20 years before leaving one of the top TV jobs in Canada—as senior producer of *Dragons' Den*—to write a novel. "It was a voice inside me telling me I had to go out on my own," Lisa says. "And that voice was getting harder and harder to ignore." I remember talking to Lisa one day after a taping—she was deeply conflicted. Raised in a working-class family, she knew the value of a good, secure job. She didn't want to leave the show—especially because she didn't have a contract for the book she wanted to write. But she had an idea for an erotic novel and, in the post–*Fifty Shades of Grey* era, knew the book had the potential to be not only a great story but also a commercial success. She needed more time to write—that meant leaving her beloved job. Many writers I know wouldn't think of mixing business and art, but Lisa has the heart of a writer and the instincts of a true entrepreneur. So I gave Lisa the best advice I could: trust your gut. She gave her notice in May and spent the summer working on her book. In September, she scored a major book deal, and her erotic novel, *S.E.C.R.E.T.*, became a huge international bestseller. When she talks about her life now, her descriptions always circle back to the most important word in an entrepreneur's vocabulary: freedom.

When you're being true to your entrepreneurial instincts, life feels almost hyper-real. Serial entrepreneur Kelsey Ramsden says she never feels as alive as she does when she's making a deal. "My heart pounds harder, I actually salivate, I'm sweating, and I have this visceral rush from creating something new. I'm all in—mind, body and soul."

When I hear these entrepreneurs describe their experiences, I feel profoundly moved, because an independent life can sometimes be a lonely one, and it just feels so good to know there are other people out there who feel exactly like I do. So many of the things entrepreneurs routinely do in order to pursue growth—cancelling appointments with friends, forgoing parental leave, cashing in the RRSPs—are deeply misunderstood by friends, families, and society at large. If, in reading this book you've taken comfort in the fact that my stories and experiences—and those of other entrepreneurs—match your own, then I have done my job. Because seriously, we can't all be crazy, growth-obsessed maniacs, can we? Okay, maybe we can. But my point is that it's comforting to know we've got a tribe that understands us.

* * *

Because of some of the networks I've formed through Venture, YouInc, *Dragons' Den*, and *The Big Decision*, I've had the opportunity to get to know hundreds of talented entrepreneurs. Few of these people made it on the basis of their business models or technical skills alone. They achieved success because they either had or developed the emotional tools they needed—the ones I've written about in this book—to build and sustain successful ventures. You can succeed in business without an MBA—but if you're starting a new venture or growing an existing one, you'll burn yourself out if you don't have the emotional fundamentals you need to underwrite your efforts.

As I mentioned in the beginning of this book, we live in the age of the celebrity entrepreneur and instant gratification. Thanks to the phenomenal success of young entrepreneurs in the technology space like Facebook's Mark Zuckerberg and Google founders Larry Page and Sergey Brin, there's an expectation that if you're going to achieve success, it's going to happen quickly.

Most overnight successes take decades (at least!) to achieve. Years before I began co-starring on *Dragons' Den*, I was pounding the pavement, poring over financial statements, hustling for clients. If I hadn't developed the emotional skills needed to sustain me, I never would have made it. Some of these fundamentals are innate—I have questioned the status quo since I was a kid, and I had the exasperated parents and teachers to prove it. But other skills—like losing my need to please people, or having the courage to deliver bad news swiftly—I've honed through two decades of making mistakes. There were many days when I wished I'd had someone to prepare me for the trials that lay ahead. It's my hope that by applying some of the lessons you've learned in this book, you can cut your learning curve a little shorter.

Our cultural fascination with entrepreneurs has resulted in a surge in entrepreneurship education programs. I'm all for education, and I aim to learn something new each day. But the irony about these courses is that they often teach the very things most successful entrepreneurs end up outsourcing anyway—accounting, innovation, HR. If we're going to take entrepreneurship seriously, we need to equip aspiring and serial entrepreneurs with the skills they'll never be able to hire out—resilience, perseverance, comfort with being misunderstood, and so on. The importance of these emotional skills can't be overstated.

And speaking of taking entrepreneurship seriously, we do need to do it more than ever before. People are still reeling from the effects of the global financial crisis. What the world needs now is economic growth and job creation. Entrepreneurs play a tremendous role in fuelling that growth. We need to support them in this crucial work. And perhaps the best way we can support entrepreneurs is to help entrepreneurs' families, friends, and communities understand why we do the so-called crazy things we do—like checking our messages during family gatherings, or leveraging the family home in order to grow the business.

We also need to support and nurture entrepreneurial instincts when we see them. While many people claim to appreciate and support entrepreneurs, often the opposite is true. When a person sees an opportunity and truly goes for it, it's easy for the people around him to feel envious, ashamed, or worried what other people will think. A friend recently told me a great story that illustrates this point. Her seven-year-old son was playing in his yard when he noticed traffic at a standstill in both directions on the road in front of his house. He asked his parents why the cars were backed up, and they told him it was because there was a major event happening up the road and the parking lots at the venue were full. "We could charge them money to park here!" he said. My friend told me her initial response was to give him a flat-out "no" because she was worried her neighbours might think she was cashing in on the situation. But she held her tongue while her husband helped their son make a sign that read: "Parking, $10." With her husband supervising, the woman watched from the window as her son held out the sign, greeted customers, and showed them where to park. He made 80 bucks in 20 minutes. He was delighted with himself, and when my friend saw her son's face flushed with pride, she was so glad she didn't shut him down for doing what entrepreneurs do every day—seeing an opportunity and seizing it.

I have faced a lot of challenges in my life—I've been divorced twice, I temporarily lost custody of my four kids, business deals have failed, I've been flat broke, I've been deeper in debt than I thought possible, and no matter how hard I train, the scale never seems to do what I want it to do. But my unhappiest times have been when I haven't honoured my entrepreneurial nature—when I've lived my life to grow someone else's vision, rather than my own.

I found my niche when I took the reins at Venture. Right away the qualities that once caused me so much strife—stubbornness, impatience, ambition, challenging the status quo—were the very characteristics my new role required. And even though it would be years before Venture became a success, almost overnight I experienced the joy and sense of belonging you get when you're doing what you were born to do.

I'm proud of the things I have accomplished in my life—the businesses I've grown, my wonderful kids and grandkids. But I'm not done yet. Not even close. I wake up every day knowing I have so much more to do, and understanding that in order to achieve the things I dream of and to have the relationships I want, there can be no half-measures or so-so commitments. I have to be all in. It's in my nature. And if you've made it with me this far, I suspect it's in yours, too.

I wish you the best of luck.

Continuing the Conversation

Throughout my journey as an entrepreneur, I have found both solace and knowledge when I've been fortunate enough to speak to, and learn directly from, other entrepreneurs. This is why I created YouInc.com, a website built by entrepreneurs for entrepreneurs. I envisioned YouInc as a virtual world where self-made men and women would encourage, celebrate, and embrace what makes entrepreneurs unique—learning from one another and achieving our greatest successes along the way.

Life is so busy when you are building a business. The lines between work life and home life blur, and the days become filled so quickly. We spend endless hours on the many issues and opportunities that come our way, and yet comparatively little time on ourselves and on the deeper thoughts and strategies that inform our daily decisions.

Nobody knows the entrepreneurial journey like another entrepreneur. YouInc provides a place for collaboration and networking, two of the founding principles of creative innovation and business success. It also provides educational tools, research, new and compelling storytelling, and most of all a community where you can share your stories and insights, your pains and your triumphs.

I am confident that YouInc will help you, as a business leader, grow and learn. I know you will feel good about helping others while you are, at the same time, helping yourself and your business. Please join. Tell us what your issues are. Ask for the advice and input you need.

Membership is free and it takes only seconds to join. We are always seeking input and advice about how to make the site better for all of us who work hard every day to build our dreams, so feel free to pass on your ideas and thoughts to us once you've joined. Also follow us on Twitter @YouInc or like us on Facebook at You Inc.

I can't wait to read your stories and learn from all of you.

Acknowledgements

The process of writing this book reflected all the highs and lows of running a new business. I went from the high-stress and high-energy phase of a start-up to wishing I had never taken this project on, to wondering if I was going to survive it, to wishing I could write three more books on the subject. There were times when I felt overwhelmed, intellectually, emotionally, and physically. But there were many more times when I knew I had no choice but to go all in and persevere. After all, I wasn't just telling my own story but the stories of many other entrepreneurs—men and women who, like me, wish they'd known more about the ups and downs of the entrepreneurial lifestyle before they found themselves living it. All of them decided to participate for one reason only: to help other entrepreneurs on their journeys.

They are the people to whom I owe the deepest debt of gratitude: the dozens of entrepreneurs, all at different stages of their own journeys, who agreed to be interviewed for this book. You know who you are, and I hope you also know that without your input and insights, your candour and courage, this book would not exist. Your willingness to reflect not just on the victories but also on the disappointments along your own paths to independence humbled and inspired me. Each of you made me see our world a little differently. Thank you, from the bottom of my heart.

Thank you also to Kate Fillion, Wendy Dennis, and Eleanor Beaton, three strong women who made this book a reality. You helped shape, inform, and tell the stories of entrepreneurs and what our lives are all about. For this, I am grateful beyond words.

Thank you to my agent, Rick Broadhead, and to my publisher, HarperCollins. Iris Tupholme listened when I insisted this book needed to be written, and my editor Kate Cassaday's passion for the subject made the book much stronger.

Thanks to the extraordinary teams at Venture Communications and Arlene Dickinson Enterprises who held down the fort as I worked through the book.

And thank you always, always, always to my family. You are the meaning of my life.